10,000 HOURS:
YOU BECOME WHAT YOU PRACTICE

PHYLLIS LANE

WITH RODRIGO COELHO

Cover design, photography,
and all original artwork by Phyllis Lane

Copyright © 2012 Phyllis Lane

All rights reserved.

ISBN: 1475033621
ISBN-13: 978-1475033625

DEDICATION

Dedicated to those who are deeply involved in learning practices that encourage good health, financial freedom, community, and a sense of oneness in the spirit of the universe.

CONTENTS

	Acknowledgments	i
	INTRODUCTION	1
1	THE KING AND THE SERVANT	10
2	THE PRACTICE EQUATION	14
3	TWO PATHS	21
4	TALENT	87
5	MASTERS/KINGS AND THEIR SECRETS	92
6	IT'S JUST A MATTER OF TIME	102
7	CHECK YOURSELF	106
8	EVERY PRACTICE MATTERS	110
9	SPIRITUAL PRACTICE	114
10	ULTIMATE PRACTICE	126
	AFTERWORD: AS YOU PRACTICE	136
	WORKBOOK	151
	RESOURCES	161

ACKNOWLEDGMENTS

I'd like to thank Rodrigo for putting "meat on the bones" of the "skeleton" I created of this book—writing, editing, and adding valuable input. He has been by my side every day for 10 years through thick and thin and has been my greatest teacher. Thank you to all of my mentoring clients, who were test beds for the refinement of this material before the book came to form, and who taught me immensely by your practices. To my parents, who taught me the invaluable lesson about discipline and practice from an early age. And to all the great mentors and teachers I've learned from over the last twenty years reading countless books in morning light. I haven't missed one day in all this time. Your words have nurtured and supported me in creating an amazing life, and I thank you all for leaving maps to the great destinations in life. Specific thanks are deserved by Michon Javelosa, Cassie Tolman, Tim Wright, SARK, Eric Maisel, Larry Winget, and Gary Fong.

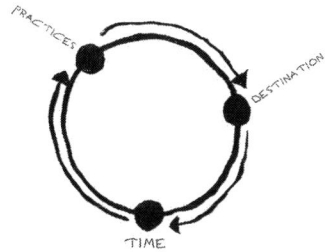

INTRODUCTION

"Everything is practice."
Pelé, Brazilian soccer phenomenon

Practice, practice, practice. Practice makes perfect. We've all heard these sayings at some point in our life. But how much have we taken them to heart?

I'm here to tell you that *practice makes everything.* YOU BECOME WHAT YOU PRACTICE. Right now you are practicing health or practicing sickness, practicing wealth or practicing poverty, practicing love or practicing fear. Every moment is declaring one path or the other . What you practice today, you become tomorrow.

You don't just wake up wealthy or wake up with cancer. The result is something you practiced every day. As a pianist, I know that if you want to play a song, you first have to figure out what song you want to learn.

Then you have to show up on the piano today to learn one measure. Then tomorrow another measure. Then another. And over time, you will have learned how to play a song, one step at a time.

In the past few years, a big wave in popular thought swept the world leading people to believe that simply thinking something would make it come to pass. Perhaps you have tried positive thinking or repeating mantras like "I am rich! I am rich! I am rich!" over and over again. Did it work? Most likely not. It's not only what you *think* today that you become, it is what you PRACTICE today that you become.

Let me first define practice.

Practice is simply an action repeated, over time.

Every day, whether we are conscious of it or not, we are practicing something.

In life, we have 3 factors that make up the life formula. The first factor is time.

TIME

When we first come into this world, we are given one gift--time. Time is the most valuable asset we don't own. What we do with our time brings us to the next factor--practice.

INTRODUCTION

PRACTICE

Our practices lead us in small increments each and every day, one step at a time, to the final factor, our destination.

DESTINATION

This book will delve more deeply into these three elements and will cover the simple daily practices that lead to great destinations in the major areas of our lives: health, wealth, relationships, spirituality, and mastery.

I can honestly say that it took over thirty years of practice to write this book about practice.

I wrote this book because I live by the words herein —I live by practicing. This isn't just small talk. I grew up on an organic apple tree farm in Oregon at the foot of the majestic Mt. Hood. In addition to tending 30 acres of trees, our family also had cows, chickens, goats, dogs, and cats to take care of. As children, we worked hard. We had many chores to do, and there was no question about doing them. In these fertile grounds, I learned the valuable discipline of taking care of things every day. You couldn't miss a day. If you did, an animal would go hungry. You couldn't be lazy, there was a job to do.

My parents instilled in me the discipline of practice. After school, I had to practice piano and finish my homework before I could go out and play. There were many days I would be on the piano looking out the window at all of the kids laughing, running, and playing outside. Oh, how I longed to join them! But rules were rules in my house, and my parents wouldn't have it. Instead, what happened after years of practicing two hours a day was that by the age of 12, I was a full-fledged concert pianist winning the Bolognini scholarship with my sights set on Juilliard.

Throughout those years, I also studied dance. Between school and practicing, my days were full. By this time, my family had moved to Las Vegas, where there were better teachers for me to learn from. I started performing on the weekends. I was part of a group called the "Young Entertainers" that would put on a show at the Tropicana. I would sing, dance, and play piano in this group.

I won a Young Miss Magazine contest at 16, and the next thing I knew signed with the Ford NY model agency. Life took on a fast pace and I was traveling a lot. I traveled to 25 different countries by the time I was 25. In Tokyo, where I spent a lot of time modeling, I picked up a Nikon FE2 and started photographing. I was 17 at the time. Some modeling friends asked me to photograph them, and you could say the rest is history. I've probably photographed 10,000 people since then, and have been dedicated to the craft. I now photograph for a lot of money, and for no money. For the wealthy, and for charity. Either way, I give all I have in the moment and I love what I do.

During my travels, I began to read inspirational books from the masters of self improvement, ancient wisdom, psychology, health, and anything else I could get my hands on. I began to journal every day. Over twenty years and perhaps 5,000 books later, I have not missed a single day in all this time. I consider my two hours in the morning my sacred time to reflect, to contemplate, to learn, and to create. I draw and practice piano as part of my daily practice. It is like a meditation. During this time, all of my great ideas have been born. I've set the course for my life, and checked in to make sure I'm still on the path. I've learned the most valuable bits of wisdom that have made all of the difference in my life. I wouldn't miss a day for anything.

A few years ago, I read *Outliers* by Malcolm Gladwell, and more recently *Finding Your Way in a Wild New World* by Martha Beck. In these books they discuss the "10,000 hour rule" which states that it takes about 10,000 hours of practice to master a skill. This idea is based on research by Anders Ericsson, who studied virtuoso violinists and other so-called "geniuses" in a range of skill areas to see if there were any brain based differences in the super talented. They discovered there isn't any neurological difference and mastery all came down to how much time practicing they put in--about 10,000 hours on average. Ten thousand hours equates to 1½ hours every day for 20 years! You can see that how after about twenty years, mastery or mediocrity begin to show up.

It's very easy to draw the parallels between practice and life. We tend to think that practice is limited to learning a musical instrument or swinging a golf club, but in fact, we are practicing every moment in all areas of life. Take our health, for instance, and apply the 10,000 hour rule to that. It is no accident that health conditions begin to show up in our 40's and 50's, because we have been practicing that ailment for over 20 years just as the rule says! We've become masters at being overweight and unhealthy, just by the small steps we've taken every day for a long period of time.

Once again it is the secret formula of

TIME + PRACTICE = DESTINATION

During this time I began mentoring other people, and I noticed that failure in life had similar patterns or practices. Although people said they wanted financial freedom or great relationships, their actions and daily practices weren't in alignment with their desired destination. They were practicing being broke and alone without knowing it. The major difference between success and failure in life is just a few basics practiced every day.

This book is a summary of what I share with my mentoring clients over the course of many one to two hour sessions. It contains a great deal of wisdom condensed into a bite size package, with enough information to whet your appetite to dig in deeper. I wish I had read this book when I got out of high school and began my own life practices.

This is not a self help book, this is a life help book. This isn't a New Age book, but a book that hopefully will carry you to old age with the life you have imagined. *10,000 Hours* is not just a spiritual book of words, but spirit, heart, mind, and feet book. We cannot leave out the feet. The feet represent the practice. These simple practices will lead you to the destination you desire. The simple steps will get you from here to there. And the truth is, you are stepping every day whether you know it or not.

If you tell me what you practiced today, I can tell you your destination. I find at the deepest level, we all want great health or great wealth, great relationships or to be great at something. Most people just think that it happens. Most people don't realize that there are only about a **handful** of practices or formulas in each of these categories that lead to greatness.

This book is about deciding where you really want to go, your destination, and the concise practices and formulas that will get you there culled from many sources and many years trying them out myself. This is a practical guide, a life alchemy book. It is the secret behind "The Secret." It's great to imagine your greatest dreams, create a vision book, but then what? It's great to use positive thinking, and mantras, but then what?

As the great success philosopher Jim Rohn said:

"Affirmation without discipline is the beginning of delusion."

We'll talk more about this later, but there are 3 SIMPLE QUESTIONS you need to ask yourself.

1. DESTINATION – where do I really want to go? Wealth, Health, Relationships, Skills

2. HOW DO I GET THERE?

3. HOW DID I GET HERE?

I hope that after reading this book, you too will decide on a destination, take up a practice, and not miss a day. You will know after finishing this book how important practice is to your life, and you will take it very seriously.

In this journey we become a master—a master over ourselves to say no to this and yes to that.

As Lao Tsu said, the journey of a thousand miles begins with one step… one step… one step…

INTRODUCTION

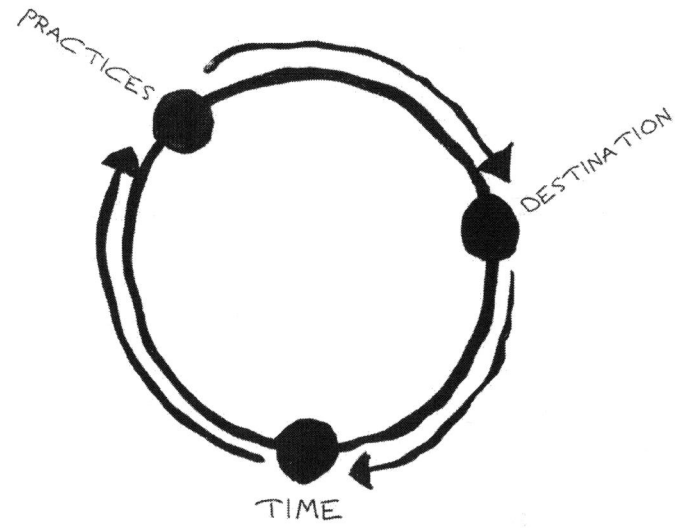

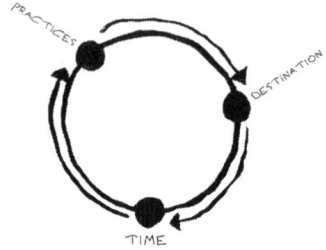

1 THE KING AND THE SERVANT

> "One must picture oneself as two beings, one the king and the other the servant. When one of them expresses a wish, it is the king who wishes; and the part that says "I cannot" is the servant. If the servant has his way, then the king is in the place of the servant. And the more the servant has his way, the more the servant rules and the king obeys. In this way naturally conflict arises inwardly and that reflects upon the outer life, making the whole life misery."
>
> *Hazrat Inayat Khan, from Mastery*

In this wonderful story, we see that there are the practices of the King and the practices of the Servant, and that these two people live in all people. The King is the visionary--he sees the bigger picture, the whole kingdom, the future destination. The King sees to it that his servants carry out his wishes. If they don't, off with their heads!

The Servant sees only himself and meeting his urgent desires in this moment. He is all for instant gratification and fun.

In neuroscience, the King represents the conscious mind, and the Servant is the subconscious mind.

So the ultimate destination in life is to become the King, the master. To become more conscious. The master over your base desires, your subconscious programming, and be the King of your life. Who do you have to become in order to reach your chosen destination? Every moment you are choosing to act out the King's orders or be distracted by giving in to the Servant's desires.

When the King is in control, the King says, "don't eat that piece of cake! I am trying to be healthy. Let's eat this kale salad instead." And the Servant obeys. When the King is not in control, and the subconscious programming takes over, the Servant says, "I'm going to eat the whole cake. Screw it. MMMMM." And right there, the King has lost some power, and on it goes until the Servant takes over the power of the King.

We need to get the King back in control of his kingdom, and the Servant to carry out the King's wishes. If man (or woman) does not realize that he is the King (or Queen) and allows the Servant, his base desires, to over rule his wishes, then the King will lose his kingdom.

From the time you are born until the age of 7, your subconscious mind is observing the practices of your caretakers, never missing anything, and deeply storing this information away. You are absorbing by witnessing the actions that are taken, and the actions you begin to take become ingrained in your mind. For the rest of your life, this programming and these practices will remain with you, unless your conscious mind, the King, steps in and creates new patterns by learning new practices.

In your life, who's in charge, the King or the Servant?

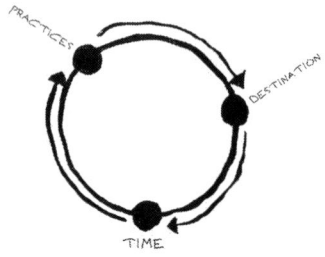

2 THE PRACTICE EQUATION

"Everything has a price. Everything has its pain. Everything is a practice."
Jim Rohn, success philosopher

TIME + PRACTICE = DESTINATION

TIME

"Time is our most valuable asset, yet we tend to waste it, kill it, and spend it rather than invest it."
Jim Rohn

All we have is the gift of time. Time is the great equalizer of mankind. Seconds slip into minutes, into hours, into days, into a lifetime. Time is neutral. It cares not what you do with it. It is entirely up to you. Today is

1440 minutes, or 86,400 ticks of the clock. We all have the same amount each day. See where you spend your time in this moment, and in this moment, and in this moment. That is all there is.

The great ones before us have shown that to become a master at anything you need to practice, it's what you do with your time that makes all the difference. Research has shown that mastery happens in practicing for:

> 10,000 hours, or
> 12 hours a day for 2.5 years, or
> 6 hours a day for 5 years, or
> 20 hours a week for 10 years, or
> 1.5 hours a day for 20 years

It's the long term that matters.

PRACTICE

Practices are what we do with our time. They are the little steps, repeated every day.

Practice creates our tomorrow whether we are aware of it or not. It is what you did when you first woke up, what you ate for breakfast, what you did at your job, whether or not you exercised, and whether you sat in front of the TV or communicated with your partner.

Every moment of every day you are practicing health or sickness, wealth or poverty, great relationships or broken relationships.

The beauty of practice is that we can learn from the practices of those who've already arrived at their desired destination.

DESTINATION

Destinations are where we end up in life. After years of practicing every day, we usually end up somewhere. Hopefully it is where we want to be. Sadly, for most, it's not. For those few who have arrived, they were clear on their destination and they defined it. That destination governed their practices every day.

Our actions are either future-backward, or past-forward. We can be proactive where our future destination dictates what we do now, or reactive, where our past programming controls our behaviors now.

To find out where you will end up (Destination), let's see what you practiced today (Practices + Time).

If you are conscious, you get to choose your destination. Otherwise your destination is chosen for you by default.

There are two kinds of people: the true masters who know where they want to go and do the right practices that get them there, and the accidental masters who find themselves in a destination where they don't want to be… a victim of their circumstance. True masters determine their destination from their higher selves—where they are going is based on the greatest vision they have for their life.

Lewis Carroll summed this up best in *Alice's Adventures in Wonderland*.

> "Would you tell me, please, which way I ought to go from here?"
>
> "That depends a good deal on where you want to get to," said the Cat.
>
> "I don't much care where--" said Alice.
>
> "Then it doesn't matter which way you go," said the Cat.
>
> "--so long as I get SOMEWHERE," Alice added as an explanation.
>
> "Oh, you're sure to do that," said the Cat, "if you only walk long enough."

You finally are on your own. And your parents hand you the keys to your new car—it's called your life. You get in your car, and it feels good. You are on your own. But as you start driving, you realize you don't know where you are going or even where you want to go! The car seems to drive itself, as if it was a robot car that had been programmed with a preset GPS roadmap.

The car has a cruise control, it makes you do certain practices—do this, don't do that—and it seems to be stopping at all the familiar places. The same places your parents stopped at. You find yourself at a place called *"poverty and struggle."* Or maybe you end up in a place called *"wealth."* It could be a place called *"mediocrity,"* or a place called *"mastery."* It could be a place called *"health"*, or a place called *"sickness."* It could be a place called *"great relationship"*, or a place called *"broken relations."*

You can say, "Well, I know these places. This is where I always went as a kid with my parents." Or you can wake up to your subconscious programming—the family practices that were programmed into you from the ages of 0 to 7. This programming is now driving the car of your life without your input. You can wake up and begin to see where you are, and what practices got you here. Decide now where you really, really want to go.

You can also just get in your car and keep going to the same places and blame your car, or the traffic. Or you can just drive around aimlessly and say, "I don't care where I go, I just want to enjoy the ride." This is okay, until you end up somewhere you don't really want to be--like overweight, with diabetes, in debt, and suffering.

OR, you can find a new map, the practices of someone who has already arrived, and choose a new destination. You can then override your automatic navigation system.

So **first**, decide right now where you want to go in these areas and what that means exactly. Define it in as much detail as you can. Always begin any journey with the end in mind.

For example, let's say:

WEALTH – your destination is Financial Freedom, where you no longer work for money but money works for you.

HEALTH – You are vibrant, alive, with lots of energy, strong and fit.

RELATIONSHIP – You have intimacy, connection, and closeness with a partner who values growth and healing of past wounds.

CREATIVITY – You have mastery of a particular skill.

SPIRIT – You are peaceful, generous, joyful, alive, caring and giving .

Make a decision that this is where you are heading, and that you are going to commit to learning and doing the daily practices that will lead you to this destination. We will get to these practices in the next chapter. The great news is that there are only a handful in each area that make all the difference.

10,000 HOURS

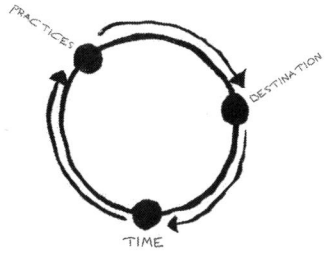

3 TWO PATHS

"There are always two choices. Two paths to take. One is easy. And its only reward is that it's easy."

Unknown

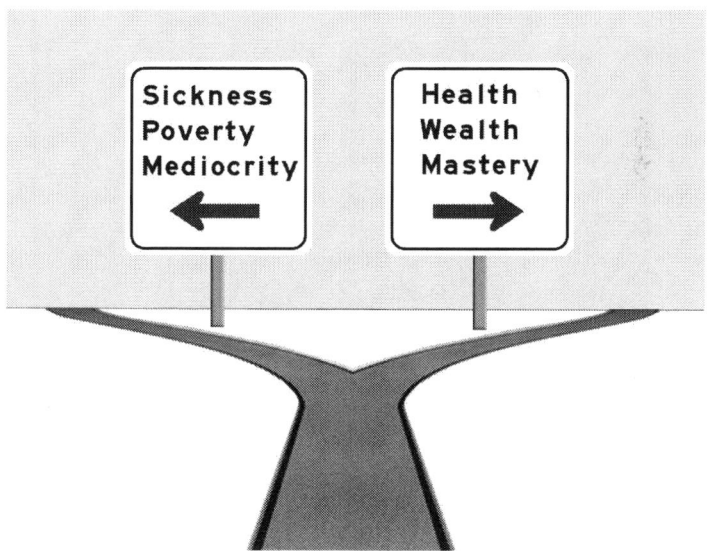

Two roads diverged in a yellow wood,
And sorry I could not travel both
And be one traveler, long I stood
And looked down one as far as I could
To where it bent in the undergrowth;

Then took the other, as just as fair,
And having perhaps the better claim
Because it was grassy and wanted wear,
Though as for that the passing there
Had worn them really about the same,

And both that morning equally lay
In leaves no step had trodden black.
Oh, I marked the first for another day!
Yet knowing how way leads on to way
I doubted if I should ever come back.

I shall be telling this with a sigh
Somewhere ages and ages hence:
Two roads diverged in a wood, and I,
I took the one less traveled by,
And that has made all the difference.

Robert Frost

There are simple practices that lead to general destinations. I will outline these practices in this chapter. It might be a good idea to bookmark the practices or write them down somewhere where you can see them to help you commit to doing them every day in a small way. The website for this book, 10000hoursbook.com, has a Wisdom Library so that you can study each of the practices in depth from other teachers. These practices have been taken from many years of study and from doing them in my own life. I have personally tested over the years what works and what doesn't. I have had failures like anyone else. I can say that these practices work.

Let's start with the practices of wealth and the practices of poverty. Which ones are you practicing now? If you find you do have some of the undesired practices, commit to making a small change in that practice. As you learned already a new practice over a long time leads to a new destination.

As you review the practices, ask yourself, "What did I practice today?"

THE PRACTICES OF WEALTH

1. Know where you want to go

2. Pay yourself first

3. Get educated

4. Know your numbers

5. Invest to make your money grow

6. Give

THE PRACTICES OF POVERTY

1. Have no idea where you want to go
2. Spend everything (or more) than you make
3. Don't know your numbers
4. Are not financially educated
5. Throw money away
6. Be stingy

THE PRACTICES OF WEALTH

"If a man is proud of his wealth, he should not be praised until it is known how he employs it."

Socrates

Know where you want to go

This almost goes without saying, but it amazes me how many people have no clue where they want to go! You wouldn't get in your car without a destination, and yet, people do it every day in other areas of their life. I sometimes ask my clients where they want to be financially in 5 years, and many of them don't know or don't have a clear answer. They may say they want to "get by" or "live comfortably", but not have a specific end in mind. That's like saying, "I'd like to get somewhere *near* Manhattan on my trip." Really!?!

"I find it fascinating that most people plan their vacation with better care than they do their lives."

Jim Rohn

The first step before embarking on any practice is to have the end in mind. It's that simple. So easy, yet so hard to do.

Right now, define exactly where you want to go financially. How much do you want to have saved? How much do you want to have invested? How much do you want to give? How much passive income do you want to generate each month from your investments?

Pay yourself first

Many people have it backwards. They pay all the bills and if there is anything left over, they either spend it all, or if they are one of the few with savings, they put some away.

The wealthy, however, do the opposite. They take a portion of every dollar that comes in and put it into different buckets for saving, investing, spending, and giving. Then, they pay the bills with what is left over. The wealthy most importantly, spend less than they earn.

Those who practice wealth have a plan, and they stick to their plan. They know where they are going, and deliberately follow the map and take the steps to get there.

Get educated

You wouldn't jump out of a plane without some expert instruction first. You could be severely injured or die if you don't. Well, people will handle money and "invest" without ever reading or learning the basics first in the same way. We all know that we are not given a financial education in school. We all have some learning to do on our own. We have to seek out the teachers and mentors who will give us this education after the school bell rings.

Let's assume you are one of the few who have followed the second practice of paying yourself first, and have managed to save some money. How many stories have we heard about people who have invested money in get rich quick schemes, let relatives borrow money never to see it again, or started businesses that they put their last dime into that failed? These are all things these people would have learned not to do had they been financially educated first.

"The book you don't read won't help."

"Miss a meal if you have to but don't miss a book."

Jim Rohn

Know your numbers

Wealthy people know where their money goes. They keep track of their expenditures and check on their statements monthly or more. They know how to read financial statements. They stay on top of their finances because they know how quickly it can be lost. Many wealthy people have lost before, and learned the painful lessons that now make them smarter with their money.

Invest to make your money grow

Wealthy people invest their money and make it grow. They treat each dollar like a seed that could potentially spout a farm of dollar trees. They get paid a return on their invested money.

You might not realize this, but simply saving up 50,000 with a 5% interest you would be earning a pretax $200 per month! See below:

$100,000 at 5% $400/month
$200,000 at 5% $800/month
$500,000 at 5% $2,000/month
$1,000,000 at 5% $4,000/month

There are many ways to make your money grow—stocks, bonds, mutual funds, commodities, real estate, business ventures, and so on. There is a difference between "good" debt and "bad" debt, just like there is a difference between a good investment and a bad investment. A financial education will teach you the difference. Robert Kiyosaki, author of the bestseller *Rich Dad, Poor Dad* explains it in the following way. Good debt "puts money in your pocket." In other words, good debt is used to buy assets like rental real estate where the tenant pays for the debt and hopefully the rent more than covers the expenses and puts money in your pocket every month. Bad debt, on the other hand, like a car payment or a credit card payment, takes money out of your pocket every month. Good debt makes you richer, bad debt makes you poorer.

Kiyosaki's rich dad said that you should treat all debt, good or bad, like a loaded gun—with a lot of respect. The wealthy know that once you take on bad debt, you have enslaved yourself and given up a portion of your future earnings from hard sweat and labor to have that one thing you couldn't resist NOW. This is what the expression the "time value of money" is all about. Money now versus money later.

Kiyosaki tells a story to illustrate good debt and bad debt. He had the desire to buy a Porsche. He had the money to pay cash for the Porsche, but instead of doing that, he went searching for a rental property. It took some time, effort, and discipline to do that. He then used the cash on a down payment on a property that would cash flow enough every month that it would cover his car loan payment.

Once he found the property, found a tenant and started creating cash flow, he went to the dealer and financed the Porsche, paid for by the real estate. He now had the car of his dreams, and slept very well knowing that in 5 years he would still own the car free and clear, still own the real estate (which most likely would have appreciated by then), and be offering up a needed place to stay for someone who couldn't or didn't want to own. There would be tax benefits too, but that is beyond the scope of this book.

There are many ways to increase your nest egg. Get educated and get you're your money growing. Once you've practiced Getting Educated, you too will understand all the benefits. Please visit the Wisdom Library at 10000hoursbook.com for more resources.

Give

I can't say that all "rich" people give, but truly wealthy people give. These people believe like I do that giving increases receiving. You may have heard the saying "you have to give to receive." Giving affirms to the universe that you have more than enough, and that you want to share your bounty with the rest of the world.

In the end, you don't take anything with you. All of your possessions are left behind. Who you have been as a person becomes your legacy. Hopefully, that is a generous and giving person.

Just look at a tree. Does it hoard or is it stingy with its fruit? No. The tree gives and gives and gives. This is the way of nature, and I have found that giving does in fact work wonders. Try it for yourself and see what happens. The receiving may not come in the same form as the giving, so if you give a flower you will not necessarily get a flower back. Be receptive to other ways you have received gifts after you give.

Warren Buffet has great wealth practices. He has an absolute passion for investing, and although he is one of the wealthiest billionaires in the world, Warren lives modestly in Nebraska in the same home he has lived in for decades and drives a Ford. It's not about the money-- he most definitely knows his numbers, and is highly financially educated. He invests for the long haul, overcoming short term distractions. He has probably spent 10,000 hours poring over financial statements. Lastly, he is a giver. He has pledged to give 99% of his wealth to charity during his life or at death, which at current values would be the largest philanthropic gift in history. As a result, he has inspired the Giving Pledge, whereby the world's richest have publicly pledged the majority of their wealth to philanthropy.

THE PRACTICES OF POVERTY

1. Have no idea where you want to go

2. Spend everything (or more) than you make

3. Don't know your numbers

4. Are not financially educated

5. Throw money away

6. Be stingy

Before I begin this section, I want to clarify one thing. When I speak about "poverty", I am referring to the state of "being broke." I realize there are billions of people throughout the world living on a dollar a day, without ready access to basic necessities, and I am not speaking here about these people living in poverty. I am referring to people who live in first world countries that have all the resources and opportunities available to them, and yet they practice daily the routines that lead them to being broke. Larry Winget, a popular "in-your-face" kind of author says it best, "You are broke because you want to be."

THE PRACTICES OF POVERTY

"Poverty is the worst form of violence."
Mahatma Gandhi

Have no idea where you want to go

Just as the wealthy know specifically what amount of wealth they wish to achieve, the poor have no idea. Some may not even consider that wealth is possible, and don't even think about it. Others might wish to be rich "one day", but really have no plan or no idea of how to get there. They haven't taken the time to read the books, study, and follow others who have already arrived.

If you do not have an idea of where you would like to be financially, if you do not come up with a number of how much you would like to have saved, how much invested, how much you are earning from your investments, and how much you would like to give, then you will always remain broke. The definition of financial independence is making enough money from your investments that they cover your monthly expenses, so you no longer have to work if you choose not to. But it first requires you to know your numbers, pay yourself first, and grow your nest egg.

Spend everything (or more) than you make

There are countless stories of lottery winners who were broke or bankrupt 5 years later, and stories of celebrities like MC Hammer who ended up broke after making millions. It would seem to be impossible starting out with millions of dollars, but the law of practice is infallible. They all spent more than they made every day. Just as night follows day, you will inevitably end up broke practicing poverty every day, no matter how much money you have. It's never about the money, it's about what you do with it. Period. How many of us have worked long hours, worked very hard, put our heart and soul into it, made lots of money, and have nothing to show for it?

You might think, how could someone spend more than they make? The answer would be, they want it now. And with credit cards, how easy? Many people spend all their cash or use credit cards for "stuff" that will take them years to pay off. There was a TV show some years ago called "Big Spender" where the host, Larry Winget, would confront people who were shopaholics and could not stop spending. Some people on the show literally had an obsessive *need* to buy something, even though they were broke. Like a heroin addict, searching for their "fix", for these people, spending was the only thing on their minds. It became a deeply ingrained pattern.

When you spend everything you make, any unforeseen necessary expenditure could wipe you out. You have no cushion. Many people who practice poverty have no health insurance. So that car accident and ambulance ride just forced them into bankruptcy. In fact, medical bills are the #1 reason for bankruptcy filings in America.

I have seen the potential damage a medical issue can cause first hand. When my partner and I were weeks into our relationship, one night he had a severe stomach pain. He went to the emergency room, and they did not diagnose it right there. Days passed and the pain got worse. By the time they figured out he had a twisted intestine, he was dehydrated and hadn't eaten. He went in for what was to be a quick surgery, but did not recover after the surgery and had to be rushed back in for emergency surgery the next day. Very long story short, he spent a month in intensive care on a ventilator in a drug-induced coma, and had to spend another month in the hospital recovering after he woke up.

He fortunately had health insurance that covered everything, but his total medical bill was over $1 million. At the time, he was in his late twenties and in great health. You would have never expected something like this to happen to someone like him. But it did. And had he not had that coverage he would have been forced into bankruptcy like millions of others.

So if you are one of those who are spending all that you make, I ask you to start taking control of your finances by writing down or tracking online how much you are spending. You absolutely must get that number to be less than you earn by any means necessary right away. Before any purchase, choice, or decision, ask yourself, "Is this supporting my destination of financial independence? Or is this taking me down the road of poverty?"

Find what frivolous expenses you have that you could live without. Do you really use that Netflix membership that is costing you $80 a year? Find ten more of these types of expenses and you've just found $800 more dollars you could put towards your financial future. I know quite a few people who got rid of their cable TV subscription and now watch the few things they were watching over the internet. This move alone could save you $500 a year or more.

It's really about becoming conscious of where you are putting your money. What you do with this $10, is what you do with $100, is what you do with $100,000, is what you do with $1,000,000. Same practice. If you can't save a dollar out of that $10, you won't do it out of a million. If you can't be a millionaire with this dollar, then you'll never become a millionaire. Many people think "when I get the money, THEN I'll start saving." It starts right now, with this dollar.

Don't know your numbers

The only way you can spend all or more than you make is by not looking at your numbers. You have no idea how much is going out and where it is going. If you did, you would know the error of your ways right away and would not let that happen. I work with many creative people, and overwhelmingly, they say they've never looked at their numbers. That is like driving with a blindfold on. It's a high risk situation, and it's going to lead to an accident at some point.

To begin walking down the road to wealth, fill out a financial statement. Visit the Wisdom Library at 10000hoursbook.com and download a template. A great suggestion is to fill out your financial statement for where you are now, and then fill out your financial statement for what you would like it to be in 5 and 10 years. That will help you get an idea for where you want to go, which is one of the practices of wealth. Then create the practice of filling out your statement once a month to see where you are at.

Another good number to know is your "wealth number." This is how many months you can live without working. Take how much you have in savings, divide by your total expenses per month, and that should give you a number. To reach financial freedom, the goal is to create the highest possible (if not infinite) wealth number.

Are not financially educated

If you do not even know what a financial statement is, or have never seen one before, don't worry. Many people haven't either. Take the time to get educated and realize that it is not going to happen overnight. You'll need to invest the time and effort into learning, but it will all be worth it. Visit the Wisdom Library at 10000hoursbook.com for suggestions on how to get started.

There are so many great teachers and mentors available today on the subject of personal finance. There is no excuse for not getting a financial education.

Throw money away

As said in the practices of wealth, "bad" debt takes money out of your pocket every month. One could call paying interest on money you have spent on material possessions, like department store credit card debt, throwing money away each month.

Back to the story about my husband and his medical issue, he was not able to work for a year after the incident, and every month his cars and his house were the hungry dragon that required feeding. He fortunately had saved up money, and that allowed him some time to recover, but he still had to quickly sell everything to stop the bad debt from sucking him totally dry.

The average credit card debt per household is $15,956. Debt is like having a leak in your boat. You are on the ocean, hoping to get somewhere, and all the while, this leak is filling your boat with water and beginning to sink your boat. As you are working hard to bail out water, you realize you aren't getting anywhere. And you realize, the bigger the debt becomes, the bigger the hole in the boat. So the first course of action is to patch that hole up.

If you are one of the many who has significant "bad debt", there are ways to get out. One way is to focus on paying off the highest interest rate credit card first while paying the minimum on your other cards. Again, many resources are available to you for this, and the Wisdom Library at 10000hoursbook.com is a good place to start. But the important thing is that you take action now to reverse the situation and begin new practices that will turn your life toward a new destination.

Be Stingy

People with a lot of money can be stingy too. No one likes a stingy person. Have you ever been out to dinner with a friend, and when the bill comes they are counting up who got dessert and who didn't? The generous thing to do would be to just split the bill and move on. If there is such a concern over a few dollars, then perhaps they should be eating ramen at home. My father was always generous with taking care of the tab at dinner--I always admired that quality.

Being stingy is reaffirming the belief that there is not enough, which goes against nature. We all have an innate desire to give of ourselves and our resources to help others. It's just how we are wired. When you cut yourself off from your true nature, the flow of good things coming your way stops. People do not want to give to you. You get what you give. So if you give little you get little in return. It's that simple.

And giving is not limited to just money, so don't feel like you can't give if you are broke. You can give of your time, your skills, your laughter, your smile. All is for giving.

> "The value of a man should be seen in what he gives and not in what he is able to receive."
> *Albert Einstein*

I make millions

I save millions

I invest millions

I give millions away

Mark Victor Hansen and Robert Allen from the One Minute Millionaire

THE PRACTICES OF HEALTH

1. Eat organic living whole foods

2. Drink lots of water, raw vegetable juices, and green tea

3. Exercise

4. Nurturance

5. No drugs/alcohol/addictions

6. Get blood work done yearly

THE PRACTICES OF DISEASE

1. Eat mostly "dead" foods
2. Drink sodas and sugary caffeinated drinks
3. Lead a sedentary life
4. Neglect nurturance
5. Do drugs and alcohol/feed addictions
6. Suppress immune system with over the counter or prescribed drugs

THE PRACTICES OF HEALTH

"The only way to keep your health is to eat what you don't want, drink what you don't like, and do what you'd rather not."
Mark Twain

Eat organic living whole foods

Countless studies have shown that the American diet, characterized as highly processed, animal product rich, sugary, fatty and salty—is bad for our health. We all know it. We've all seen it. There are more obese people now than ever and it's a result of the food we are eating. Those that practice health eat primarily a plant-based diet of living foods rich in vitamins, minerals, and enzymes. They eat all colors of the rainbow from a variety of fresh, alive, organic fruits and vegetables. Living, or raw, foods are those that have not been cooked, processed, or treated with pesticides or herbicides. They represent the unbroken wholeness of original creation.

Some studies say that 80% of the diet should be plants, with the remaining 15% from grains and 5% meats (if you eat meat). Most Americans have that reversed. I can't advocate what is right for you, but there is a wealth of knowledge on this subject you should dive into, again the Wisdom Library at 10000hoursbook.com is a good start.

I really like Michael Pollan's simple advice:

"Eat food. Not too much. Mostly plants."

Every morning I use my Vitamix® blender to mix up a variety of raw vegetables, fruits, nuts and superfoods into a thick smoothie that delivers an easily assimilated concoction of concentrated vitamins, minerals, fiber and enzymes to every cell in my body. The high-speed blending condenses the volume of food I would otherwise not be able to eat if I were chewing each piece, one by one.

The plant based diet is highly alkaline. The delicate acid-alkaline balance of the body has been found to be extremely important in health, and the body is very sensitive to its pH level. The typical American diet is acid-forming. Acidosis is not in itself a specific disease; it is a general condition of the blood and thus the root of many different diseases such as diabetes, high blood pressure, cancer, tumors, and more. Many people today have this blood condition without knowing it.

Drink lots of water, raw vegetable juices, and green tea

We all know that we should drink more water. We are mostly water and if you've ever seen a stagnant pool in a drying stream bed, you know how gross that can be. Water flushes and cleanses us. And if we don't eat enough vegetables (many of us don't), vegetable juices are the next best thing.

Consuming fresh raw vegetable juice regularly can be one of the fastest ways to create vibrant health. Fresh juice has many benefits due to its alkaline nature, abundant enzymes, and other live ingredients.

Many studies have come out about the benefits of drinking green tea. It is chock full of antioxidants and compounds that potentially fight cancer and heart disease, lower cholesterol, burn fat, prevent diabetes and stroke, and stave off dementia.

While to many the jury is still out, it is better to err on the safe side and drink it anyway. Green Tea gives a wonderful mental boost without the jittering effects of caffeine. I would know, as I drank coffee every day for years and years until I found green tea. I now drink loose leaf green tea every day several times a day.

I also drink wheatgrass and coconut water, as those juices contain amazing health benefits as well. I am fortunate to live close to a vegan restaurant called Pomegranate Café that serves young coconuts from Thailand. You can drink the water, crack it open and scoop out the delicious fleshy white coconut from the inside. It is my dessert!

"Let thy food be thy medicine, and thy medicine be thy food."

Hippocrates

Exercise

We exercise not just to look good and feel good, but because it is the primary form for the body to circulate blood and oxygen. Exercise eliminates stagnancy, or toxic metabolic wastes via the lymphatic system. When the oxygen content in and around the cells of our body are optimum, disease symptoms do not manifest. Viruses, parasites, and fungi thrive in an oxygen-deficient (anaerobic) environment. Dr. Otto Warburg discovered that cancer cannot thrive in the presence of oxygen. Having a highly acidic system also decreases oxygen levels.

Today, I do 20 minutes of aerobic activity 3 times a week, flexibility/yoga once a week, and strength/resistance training once a week. I do all this at home, it's not hard core, but done as a health practice. I look at it as maintenance of my temple, and it actually gives me more energy.

Nurturance

The body needs nurturance. Just as important as it is to get your body moving through regular exercise, the body needs sufficient rest, massage, sleep, etc. to restore its energy. We assist the body in repairing itself and eliminating toxins when we get adequate rest, massage, steam baths, and quiet time. We reduce negativity, anxiousness, and stress, which cause the body to become acidic.

In my late twenties, I began to take quiet solitary retreats in nature, get regular massages, meditate, and to focus on getting a good night's rest. I added regular detoxification through steam baths or hot baths with Epsom salts. As a result of these practices, I am more balanced and calm in my everyday life.

No drugs/alcohol/addictions

This almost goes without saying, but you can't be practicing health if you are drinking, smoking, or doing drugs. Period.

Get blood work done yearly

Having my blood work done and checked once a year tells me that I'm staying on the right path. The blood test is an excellent way, like weighing yourself, to get a gauge of your overall health. It also is a way to detect health problems early. For instance, you can see in your blood if you are mineral deficient, and make necessary adjustments before it adversely affects your health. I learned the value of this from my husband, who at one time was very tired and irritable and a blood test revealed that he was anemic. He made some dietary changes and reversed this condition in a matter of weeks, which a follow up blood test revealed.

Without that blood test, one might have thought it was something else, or even worse, might have started to take over-the-counter pills or started to drink more caffeine to combat the low energy. The underlying problem would have worsened.

THE PRACTICES OF DISEASE

1. Eat mostly "dead" foods
2. Drink sodas and sugary caffeinated drinks
3. Lead a sedentary life
4. Neglect nurturance
5. Do drugs and alcohol/feed addictions
6. Suppress immune system with over the counter or prescribed drugs

THE PRACTICES OF DISEASE

"An ounce of practice is worth tons of preaching."
Mahatma Gandhi

Eat mostly "dead" foods

If you want to be sick and unhealthy, just keep eating like the typical American. Eat cooked, man-made, fast food.

If you want to be healthy, then look at what you are putting in your mouth every day and make a decision that your health is worth it to change for the better. A good way to start on the path to health is to give up white flour and sugar. Then start to add more vegetables and fruits into your diet. Enjoy a salad daily. Try to include at least one raw vegetable with each meal.

Michael Pollan has come up with 7 rules for eating:

1. Don't eat anything your great grandmother wouldn't recognize as food.

2. Don't eat anything with more than 5 ingredients, or ingredients you can't pronounce.

3. Stay out of the middle of the supermarket; shop on the perimeter of the store. Real food tends to be out the outer edge of the store.

4. Don't eat anything that won't eventually rot. There are exceptions, like honey, but things like Twinkies that never go bad aren't food.

5. Always leave the table a little hungry.

6. Enjoy meals with the people you love.

7. Don't buy food where you buy your gasoline. In the U.S., 20% of food is eaten in the car.

Drink sodas and sugary caffeinated drinks

Here are 6 ways soda ruins your health:

1. The pH of soda = pH of Vinegar. If you put soda or vinegar on metal, it will rust quickly. It takes 32 glasses of water to neutralize one can of soda.

2. Soda will leach calcium from your bones because the body is trying to neutralize the acid.

3. Soda will dissolve your tooth enamel.

4. You'll probably be fatter. According to research in the Nurses' Health Study, a single soda every day of the week (practice), added 10 pounds over a four-year period.

5. You're at risk of developing diabetes. In a study, women who drank one or more servings a day of

sugar-sweetened soda were twice as likely to develop type 2 diabetes.

6. The Nurses' study found that women who drank more than two sodas per day have a 40% higher risk of heart attacks or death from heart disease than women who didn't drink them.

Diet soda isn't any better. Several studies suggest that diet sodas have some of the same effects on health as regular sodas. To neutralize the acid condition, your body releases minerals like iodine, a low iodine condition in turn affects Thyroid health, which in turn affects metabolism, which in turn causes weight gain. It's like a gateway drug. It's a practice that leads you to sickness.

We already spoke about the importance of alkalinity to the body in preventing disease, so why would you pour acid into your body? Another note, orange juice from concentrate that has been pasteurized is acid-forming. The juice from a freshly squeezed orange is actually alkaline. Please read further from the great books in the Wisdom Library on this critical subject of acid/alkaline balance.

Lead a sedentary life

When you don't move, you stagnate. Bacteria, virus, fungi, yeast, and cancer cells thrive and reproduce in a low oxygen, decreased electron, acidic body environment. Many diseases are linked to a lack of movement. A fundamental principle of life is movement and growth. If you aren't growing, you are dying. Many of us sit at computers or TVs for long hours, and little do we know that this is one of the key practices to sickness.

So get up and move! Turn on some music and dance around the room. Even 5 minutes of brisk walking is a great start. Get some fresh air and some sunlight on the body. We live by sunlight. If you think about it, all of our food's energy comes from the sun. Whether we eat plants or grains that converted sunlight to energy, or eat animals that ate plants, the original energy came from the sun.

There's one more thing about sunlight—it's how we get vitamin D. A few years ago, vitamin D was nothing more than calcium's wingman. With no offense to vitamin C, new research suggests that vitamin D may be one of the best vitamins of all for your body. It affects cell death and proliferation, insulin production, and even the immune system. Experts believe that up to 77 percent of Americans are D deficient. And the best way to get vitamin D is via sunlight.

We live on light and oxygen! Get outside and get moving! You will feel better immediately!

Neglect nurturance

I am sure at some point you have experienced life as busy, busy, busy, sometimes with seemingly no end. I myself tended to lean towards being a Type A personality. I grew up as a hard worker, and continue to be one. But I've learned how to balance. In this culture, we tend to be more Yang-focused, neglecting our Yin nature.

Many women have a tendency to neglect themselves, always taking care of others and putting the needs of others first. Although seemingly noble, this act does no one a favor. A great illustration is what flight attendants instruct us to do on every flight. Put the oxygen mask on yourself first, and then put it on your child. Simple but powerful advice, because you would be no help to anyone if you were suffocated and unconscious from lack of oxygen!

Many men too put their work first and self care last. We all experience natural ebbs and flows of work and rest, bursts of activity and then slower periods. I advocate taking small amounts of time daily for nurturance. Take a quiet walk in nature. Even take a minute to close your eyes and follow your breath. Read from inspirational texts in the morning to start your day. You don't need to take a two week silent retreat. It's the small things added up over a long period of time that make a larger difference over the course of a lifetime.

Those that neglect this practice pay the price in the form of stress, adrenal exhaustion, and other maladies which will increase acidity and force your body to stop and rest. Listen to what your body is telling you, and give it what it needs. All pain or symptoms are a signal from your body's innate intelligence telling you that you are not in balance. Make sure you listen.

Do drugs and alcohol/ feed addictions

I have seen first hand the damage from drug and alcohol addictions. A few years ago, I did a photojournalism project on the streets with the homeless. Once a week I met with the same group of people. They wrote and shared their stories with me.

Two of them stood out to me--Papa Red and Billy. Both of them were very intelligent and well spoken, but you could see the physical toll that life had taken on them. They both had rotten and missing teeth, were underweight, and had aged well beyond their years. They had families and children, but hadn't seen them in a long time.

Overwhelmingly, many of the people I spoke to were homeless and on the streets was due to addictions. Primarily crack, and following that was alcohol. These people had let the Servant take over their lives, and as a result, they had lost their kingdom.

It's not just drugs and alcohol that cause problems, but any sort of addiction. Food addiction, sex addiction, shopping addiction, video game addiction, etc. are all damaging. Addiction is a way to deal with life. You are practicing illness, and maybe not today, maybe not tomorrow, but one day you will reach the inevitable destination from your practices. The best advice is to become conscious of your practices, and if you think you might have some sort of addiction, please seek help. There are resources available in the Wisdom Library at 10000hoursbook.com.

Suppress immune system with over the counter or prescribed drugs

Many people only go to the doctor when there is a crisis. Their practices have led them to a destination, and it is do or die. Prevention is the best cure. If you haven't had a blood test in a long time, or ever, make it a point to get one as a part of your health practice. You'll be able to see if you are on the right track or not.

The nation's multi billion dollar drug industry has us all believing that synthetic chemicals mixed in a lab are better for us than what nature has provided. Millions are taking pills every single day, shutting down their natural processes and producing side effects that are sometimes worse than the original problem. For example, over-the-counter cold medicines suppress the body's natural processes of detoxifying itself. We should honor this process—one great way is sweating through the use of hot baths. Many cultures around the world use hot mineral baths as a healing practice.

I highly recommend watching the documentary film "Fat, Sick, and Nearly Dead". In it, the main character, Joe Cross, is overweight and on a list of pills for chronic ailments. He reverses his condition through diet alone (actually going on a 90-day vegetable juice fast), and is monitored by his doctor through the entire process. He weans off medications until he no longer needs them, and his rashes and chronic conditions completely vanish. All from diet! Plants solved what pills could not.

In the film, Joe related the following information. When we were a kid and we fell down and scraped our knee, what did we do? We let the body's innate natural intelligence take over, and if we left it alone, it would do its job. Well, why don't we do the same thing on the inside of our bodies? If we just give it the right ingredients, then it will do the right thing and take care of us. In the film, you see first hand a morbidly obese person completely turn his life around with just diet and exercise.

There is a fierce debate between those who believe that genetics predetermines your fate, and those who don't believe it. I tend to stand in the middle. The cutting edge science of **Epigenetics** states that environmental factors and your choices (practices) can influence and alter the way our genes are expressed, making even identical twins different. Put another way:

While your genes may have predisposed you to a certain condition, your practices take precedence and ultimately determine how you turn out.

Please underline this! That is the message of this book! You ultimately have control over your destination, and not even your genes make you a victim to circumstance.

Isn't that inspiring? So get going and take charge of your life!

THE PRACTICES OF GREAT INTIMATE RELATIONSHIPS

1. Understand the purpose of intimate relationships

2. Have a mutual destination

3. Communicate daily

4. Resolve problems quickly

5. Spend quality time together

6. Give positive daily feedback

THE PRACTICES OF BROKEN INTIMATE RELATIONSHIPS

1. No commitment

2. No vision

3. No communication

4. Inability to resolve problems

5. No focus on working on relationship

6. Focus on what's wrong

THE PRACTICES OF GREAT INTIMATE RELATIONSHIPS

> "In a relationship each person should support the other; they should lift each other up."
> *Taylor Swift*

Before I begin this section I want to make one important point. **You don't marry a person, you marry their practices.** When you move in with someone, you are moving in with someone who makes the bed or doesn't, who leaves the toilet seat up or not, who communicates or not, and so on. It's their practices (that they learned from childhood) that you have to deal with, not the person. So by understanding the right practices and being conscious, you can work together to create new practices that long term will lead to a fulfilling relationship.

Understand the purpose of intimate relationships

No one teaches us how to have great intimate relationships. Many people simply think that relationships are just supposed to work. Those of us who have been in long-term relationships know that they are WORK. They do not just happen. And like anything else, it takes care, maintenance and daily practices to make them successful.

One of the first things that is important to understand is that we enter intimate relationships to heal our childhood wounds, evolve, and awaken.

Harville Hendrix is a relationship therapist who created the "Imago" theory. This theory states that we attract the perfect partner in our lives that mirrors the qualities we both admired and hated in our parents, and mirrors back the qualities we have disowned in ourselves. Romantic love is the door to a committed relationship and/or marriage and is nature's way of connecting us with the perfect partner for our healing.

"Every relationship is a mirror in which we learn to see and embrace all that we are: the parts of self that we like and admire and the parts that we judge and detest."
Paul Ferrini

We move into a "power struggle" soon after we make a commitment to our partner. The power struggle is necessary, for embedded in a couple's frustrations lies the information for healing and growth. This is the opposite of what society teaches us. We learn that if a couple does not fight, then they have a good relationship. It is quite the opposite, conflict is normal and healthy in relationship. If a couple does not fight, that is a good sign that they have become "parallel", which means that they have resigned themselves to not dealing with problems and not telling each other the truth.

The goal of a conscious relationship is to align our conscious mind, which usually wants happiness and good feelings, with the agenda of the unconscious mind, which wants healing and growth. This cannot happen through insight alone. Specific daily practices are necessary to shift us from having an unconscious relationship to a conscious relationship, like checking on your vision daily, having real communication daily, and getting to the core issues.

Have a mutual destination

As stated in the previous practices on wealth, you've got to know where you are going first. So one of the first things to do as a couple is to write a mutual relationship destination that honors each others values. A shared vision is what you and your partner agree on, what is important in your relationship and where you want to go. The vision should be in the form of present tense action statements, like "We communicate openly and honestly", or "We have a weekly date night", or "We share responsibilities around the house", "We respect one another", etc. The vision should be posted somewhere that you can see it daily so that you are reminded of the actions and practices that create the relationship you desire.

Communicate daily

We are also not taught how to communicate effectively. Usually we have a monologue, listening to ourselves think of what to say in retaliation to what our partner is saying.

Dr. Hendrix outlines a process called the "Imago Dialogue" which involves one partner speaking and the other partner intently listening. The listener then repeats back what was said, validates what was said, and then finally empathizes with the partner's feelings.

The steps are as follows:

1) With your partner, decide who will be the sender and who will be the receiver.

2) Sender: Say a simple sentence that begins with the word I and describes a thought or feeling. For example: *"I feel mad that you look at your phone when I'm talking to you."*

3) MIRRORING: The Receiver paraphrases your partner's message and asks for clarification. For example: *"You get mad when I look at my phone when you are talking. Did I get that right?"*

   Sender: If your partner did not paraphrase you accurately, help clarify your understanding. Keep repeating sending and paraphrasing until the Sender feels completely understood.

   Once the Receiver has gotten the message, Sender: Acknowledge that what you said, thought, and felt was accurately communicated. For example: *"Yes, I feel heard."*

4) VALIDATION: The Receiver now validates your partner's message, whether or not you agree.

For example: *"I can see that. I get it. That makes sense to me."*

5) EMPATHY: The Receiver empathizes with your partner by imagining how your partner feels about the situation described.
For example: *"I can imagine how mad you must have felt. You might have felt not loved, or that you didn't matter to me."*

6) Switch roles, and repeat Steps 1-5.

Some people in his workshops report that after practicing this dialogue with their partner they felt as if they were finally heard by their partner for the very first time. Oprah Winfrey has said after having Harville on her show that she realized that at their core, people just want to be validated. After interviewing thousands of people over many years, she finally got that people want to hear/feel this from another: **"I see you. I hear you. I feel you. And you matter."** This exercise does just that.

Resolve problems quickly

**I felt angry toward my friend.
I told my wrath. My wrath did end.
I felt angry toward my foe.
I told him not. My wrath did grow.**
William Blake

We've all heard the expression "nip it in the bud." Well, you can apply this to relationships and problem solving. Resolving issues quickly will not be hard if you are practicing daily communication. It is during this time that you can air out your frustrations, speaking honestly, being heard, coming to a resolution quickly, and forgiving. This practice will prevent you from letting upsets fester and build into resentments. Deep-Seated resentment is a major cause of relationship discord.

How we handle moments of disconnection is as important as how we handle moments of connection. When conflicts and problems go unresolved they worsen and eventually undermine the quality of the relationship. They grow like weeds and eventually choke the flowering plant that is your relationship.

Spend quality time together

Part of my relationship vision is to spend quality time together with my partner. We both work at home and own a business together, so we are physically in each other's presence most of the time. So even though we may be in proximity, it doesn't mean that we are giving each other our full undivided attention. It is important to set aside time as a practice to rekindle a connection to each other. Many couples practice a "date night", which can be a fun way to share bonding experiences. We can all get caught up in the day to day hubbub of life, like our smartphones and email, and forget to share intimacy with the one we love.

Give positive daily feedback

It is reported that most people hear one positive for every 5 negatives in relationship. Isn't that amazing? See if it is true for you. It can be easy to focus on what is wrong rather than what is right, and complain about this or that. But if you make a list of the qualities you like about your partner and make a commitment to at least once a day share what you like about them or share something they did that day that you liked, you will find that your relationship may take a turn for the better.

One of our core needs is to feel loved and appreciated, and words have the power to heal us. Each of us has a unique way in which we like to receive love, and for you, words may not make a difference. According to Gary Chapman, author of *The Five Love Languages*, the primary ways in which we express or receive love are:

1. Words of Affirmation—hearing the words "I love you" are important to you, and insults can leave you shattered.

2. Quality Time—having your partner be there with the TV off and the cell phone off and all set aside makes you feel special, and distractions or postponed dates can be hurtful.

3. Receiving Gifts—receiving a gift or gesture makes you feel that you are known and cared for, and a missed birthday or anniversary could be disastrous.

4. Acts of Service—having your partner ease your burden, or saying "Let me do that for you", would speak volumes. Laziness, broken commitments, and making more work for you tell you that you don't matter.

5. Physical Touch—you are very touchy--hugs, pats on the back, and holding hands are all very important to you. Neglect or abuse can be unforgivable and destructive.

I encourage you to read Gary's book, or take the assessment on his website to determine which is your love language and have your partner do the same. Then make a daily commitment to share your chosen act of love with your partner daily. It will make a dramatic difference in your life. I can tell you from experience that you may have health and wealth, but if your intimate relationship is broken, you will not be happy. It is critical to apply the practices to this part of your life for your overall well-being.

THE PRACTICES OF BROKEN INTIMATE RELATIONSHIPS

1. No commitment

2. No vision

3. No communication

4. Inability to resolve problems

5. No focus on working on relationship

6. Focus on what's wrong

THE PRACTICES OF BROKEN INTIMATE RELATIONSHIPS

No commitment

One of the first steps required in creating an intimate relationship is to make a commitment to one another. This is usually memorialized in a wedding, but it doesn't necessarily have to be. You and your partner can make a mutual commitment to one another on your own, without the expenditure of a big wedding. I did this with my partner, and we have been together for 10 years and counting. What is important is the decision that you are 100% in, and that you aren't going to back out when times get hard. It's a promise you intend to keep, no matter what. Only then can you move on to building an intimate relationship, because only then does each partner feel safe with unearthing deep-seated wounds.

If you are in a long term relationship without a commitment, with one foot in and one foot out, I can tell you that it won't work. We already face an uphill battle, with over 50% of marriages ending in divorce. Once a partnership has reached the power struggle phase, that's when the real work begins. Being 100% in means you are going to take responsibility and do the work.

If you are in a marriage or committed partnership and are wanting to create an amazing relationship, then I encourage you to study those who have great relationships and to begin new practices. If your partner is unwilling to join you in making the leap to a conscious partnership, you may be faced with the decision of having to leave. Regardless, studying this information will bring you great self-awareness and will help your relationship whether or not your partner contributes. As Gandhi said, "You must be the change you want to see in the world." So if you start to change for the better with new practices, you may just inspire your partner to follow suit.

No vision

As said in Proverbs 29:18, "Where there is no vision, the people perish…" The same goes for relationships. Where there is no vision, the relationship perishes. The same could be said for many other areas of life. So an important step is to create a vision of your ideal relationship with your partner and work together in small ways daily to make it the way you want it to be.

See it as it is. Not worse.

See it better than it is.

Make it the way you see it.
Tony Robbins

The vision is the map you refer to when you get lost. You can check in with your map daily as a reminder of what practices to practice.

No communication

You know you have a communication breakdown when you feel like you cannot tell your partner the whole truth. Maybe you are afraid to tell your partner the truth, because in the past you experienced abandonment. Somewhere along the way you learned that if you told the truth, you would be left alone. Pain is associated with it. Perhaps you have changed yourself into the person you think your partner wants you to be, and as a result you aren't being true to yourself. Whatever the reason, a breakdown in truthful communication is the beginning of the breakdown of a relationship.

If you are committed to your relationship working, then you must learn the skills it takes to communicate properly. It takes practice to make this work, but it will be worth the effort in the end.

Inability to resolve problems

This follows from lack of communication. You let problems linger and try to "sweep them under the rug." You ignore problems that are there. You are not seeing it as it is, perhaps you are in denial. As Paul Ferrini said, "Living with someone is like being in a pressure cooker. We are going to get cooked all the way through whether we like it or not." Ignoring problems is the fastest way to get cooked.

You and your relationship are either growing or dying. An inability to resolve problems leads to a relationship going "parallel". You and your partner are more like roommates just getting by. Once a relationship has gone parallel, it has begun the descent to death. It is no longer alive and thriving. The deep-seated resentments and unresolved problems cut off the life force of the connection like a tourniquet squeezing a vein.

No focus on working on relationship

This goes back to not understanding why we are in intimate relationships, and thinking that they should just work on their own. Many people marry before fully knowing who they are individually, and jump right into having children. Then, unfortunately, the children are caught in the power struggle of their parents and learn by osmosis how to have a bad relationship. They are programmed, and so the cycle continues. Only through educating ourselves on how to make relationships work by reading books like these, and through professional coaching and therapy that we can end the cycle of broken relationships.

Relationships are the greatest transformational tool. They are here to show us to ourselves. And if we take responsibility, we can evolve and become a more loving human being. We can grow up.

Focus on what's wrong

We have a choice about how we perceive. The other night I had a disagreement with my partner. We came to realize that what stood between us was just a story. He had placed a story of "I never do anything right" between us and he realized he had placed this story in many different areas. Now we have a new practice. Before we say something, we say, "The story I'm making about this is: _____"

Byron Katie has a great saying that we only do three things in life: we sit, we stand, and we lay. The rest we make stories about.

When you focus on what's wrong, it's really just a story. But it's a story of your own making, that you can rewrite.

THE PRACTICES OF MASTERY

1. READ / STUDY

2. Commit to practice

3. Never quit

4. Overcome resistance

5. Keep your word

6. Be 100%

THE PRACTICES OF MEDIOCRITY

1. Don't read / study
2. Practice occasionally, leisurely, or not at all
3. Quit when it gets hard
4. Skip the hard work now for pleasure
5. Break your promises
6. Be 50%

THE PRACTICES OF MASTERY

"If people knew how hard I worked to get my mastery, it wouldn't seem so wonderful at all."
Michaelangelo

READ / STUDY

I put this in all caps because I cannot emphasize enough the importance of this. The fact that you are reading this book already puts you in the top 5% of all people. Really! Ask 5 people around you what book they have read in the last 90 days and most will tell you that they haven't read one.

"Not all readers are leaders, but all leaders are readers."
Harry Truman

ALL masters have undertaken study of their skill or vocation from a teacher, mentor, coach, and/or from books. So if you aren't reading and studying from masters, you can never be one. Period.

A word of caution: reading can be another way of avoidance. It has been called "analysis paralysis." You spend so much time studying and trying to know everything you can before you start that you never start! So along with reading and study, you must apply what you learn and practice it. Knowledge without application is useless.

I can do without many possessions, but one thing I cannot do without is books. I read a book or two a week, and I am passionate about learning, and growing. My books are like mentors to me. My library of books is one of my life's treasures.

> **"The man who doesn't read good books has no advantage over the man who can't read them."**
> *Mark Twain*

Commit to practice

A common trait of masters is a commitment to every day practice.

> **"If I miss a day of practice, I know it. If I miss two days, my manager knows it. If I miss three days, my audience knows it."**
> *André Previn, conductor, composer, pianist*

We tend to only see the end result when we watch masters in action. How easily gymnasts fly through the air, or pianists play complex pieces, or artists make masterworks. What we do not see are the 10,000 hours of hard work that went into that one moment. The performance itself is a continuation of daily practice, only in front of an audience.

Mass media tends to communicate quick fixes and instant gratification. It communicates learning as linear or instantaneous, which is not reality at all. We learn in steps, we plateau for a while, and then have a leap up in skill level.

Never quit

Another universal trait of masters is perseverance. To push through 10,000 hours of practice requires great steadfastness and a steel resolve to never quit. As Winston Churchill said, "Never, never, never quit." How long do you go? UNTIL.

> **"Fall seven times, stand up eight."**
> *Japanese Proverb*

> **"It's not that I'm so smart, it's just that I stay with problems longer."**
> *Albert Einstein*

Overcome resistance

Masters have the ability to set aside the Servant voice inside them that says "Not today", called Resistance, and push through that time and time again. They are the Kings of their kingdoms.

> **"You are the knight. Resistance is the dragon."**
> *Steven Pressfield, from Do the Work*

We all face resistance. If you have a head, then you have resistance. Chatter is resistance. Resistance is sneaky and will do everything it can to keep you from practicing today. To be a master, you must be vigilant and stay on guard.

Keep your word

Keeping your word is one of the most profound practices any single person can undertake. Just this practice alone has the ability to transform your life. Keeping your word with others will make you trustworthy, and will draw opportunities to you because others will know you are a person of your word.

Masters are all skilled in keeping their word to themselves. When they say, "I'm going to practice tomorrow at 6 AM", they mean it, and all the cells in their bodies know they mean it. Resistance has no chance with someone who will keep their word no matter what.

Keeping your word is integrity. Integrity means "being whole." Being whole is your true nature.

Be 100%

In my photography career, I sometimes do free photo shoots for my personal work to fill out my portfolio. Whether it's a free shoot or a paid shoot, I approach it with the same focus and intensity. The money makes no difference to what I bring to the table in the moment, and to what level I perform. I hold myself to this standard always.

Once I was inspired to do a photo shoot with model and a giraffe that looked like it was shot in Africa. Well, I live in Phoenix, and it's a little difficult to find a giraffe with the perfect background. I pushed myself to find a location in which I would be able to pull this shot off. It took time and effort. I drove to Sedona two hours away to a wildlife park to scope it out. It ended up not working out there, but I eventually got through to the right person at the Phoenix Zoo. It took some convincing, and required getting a certain vaccination to be in the pen with the animals, but in the end I was able to get the pictures taken. And they came out amazing so it was worth it. You can check them out at phyllislane.com/giraffe.

Push yourself always to be better. To be excellent. To do the very best you can. Why become great? Why go the distance? Because you can. Greatness is in all of us.

"Being willing to see just how far you can go is the self-surpassing quality that we human beings are stuck with. Evolution is a whole long story of mastery. It's being real. It's being human. It' s being who we are."

George Leonard

THE PRACTICES OF MEDIOCRITY

1. Don't read / study
2. Practice occasionally, leisurely, or not at all
3. Quit when it gets hard
4. Skip the hard work now for pleasure
5. Break your promises
6. Be 50%

THE PRACTICES OF MEDIOCRITY

Don't read or study

You aren't practicing mediocrity right now, because you are reading this book. So I know you are doing a master's practice right now. Keep it up!

If you don't have instruction, chances are you could be practicing the wrong things. Then you perfect doing something wrong. If you play music, you know that if you learn the wrong notes, it takes twice as long to learn it the right way. It's like taking the dirt road to your destination instead of the highway. A teacher or mentor can show you the right way, or a faster way. It saves a lot of time.

Practice occasionally, leisurely, or not at all

In his profound book, *Mastery*, George Leonard outlines three types of people: the Dabbler, the Obsessive, and the Hacker. Most of us fall into one of these three categories.

The **Dabbler** tries many things, gets improvement, plateaus, gets bored, and then tries something new.

The **Obsessive** is purely results oriented. They are inconsistent and when they hit a plateau they quit because their results aren't increasing linearly.

The **Hacker** is content where he's at. He becomes proficient then doesn't care to continue improving.

There's nothing wrong with being any of these. Everyone is sometimes all of them. But if you want to become a master at anything, you must stay on the path of mastery. Mastery IS practice. It is showing up every day to do the work.

Quit when it gets hard

The path to mastery will become difficult. But how you deal with adversity will determine the outcome of your life.

I guarantee that if you practice quitting, then your life is mediocre.

Skip the hard work now for pleasure

If you've read this far, you already know about the Servant and about Resistance. You know that short term pleasure will lead to long term pain. Your work now will lead to long term fulfillment. So do the hard work now.

Break your promises

Just as keeping your word is one of the most profound practices any single person can undertake, breaking your promises will just as sure lead you down a path of mediocrity. We all know what it feels like when someone breaks their promise to us; it doesn't feel good at all. Sometimes we get angry at them. It feels twice as bad when you break promises to yourself.

I'm not saying never break your promises. Things happen in life that may prevent you from keeping your word. It's life. But there is a proper way to handle it. If you have an agreement with someone that you cannot fulfill, like showing up on time, let them know right away, and then make a new agreement with them that you will keep. Then do everything in your power to make sure that you come through on that commitment.

Be 50%

I can't imagine what it would be like to live a life where I had one foot in and one foot out. When you put 100% in, you get 100% back. When you put 99% in or less, you get nothing back. You are sending a message out to the universe that you aren't really in.

Here's a great story that illustrates this point:

An elderly carpenter was ready to retire. He told his employer-contractor of his plans to leave the house-building business to live a more leisurely life with his wife and enjoy his extended family. He would miss the paycheck each week, but he wanted to retire. They could get by.

The contractor was sorry to see his good worker go and asked if he could build just one more house as a personal favor. The carpenter said yes, but over time it was easy to see that his heart was not in his work. He resorted to shoddy workmanship and used inferior materials. It was an unfortunate way to end a dedicated career.

When the carpenter finished his work, his employer came to inspect the house. Then he handed the front-door key to the carpenter and said, "This is your house... my gift to you."

The carpenter was shocked!

What a shame! If he had only known he was building his own house, he would have done it all so differently.

So it is with us. We build our lives, a day at a time, often putting less than our best into the building. Then, with a shock, we realize we have to live in the house we have built. If we could do it over, we would do it much differently. But you cannot go back. You are the carpenter, and every day you hammer a nail, place a board, or erect a wall. The practices you do today, help build the "house" you will live in tomorrow. Whatever you do, do it wholeheartedly, like it's yours.

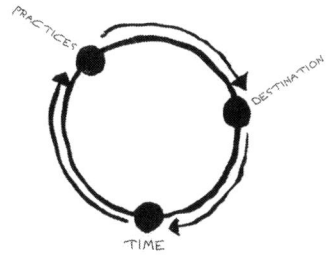

4 TALENT

"Talent is cheaper than table salt. What separates the talented individual from the successful one is a lot of hard work."

Stephen King

Contrary to popular belief, people are not born with the natural talent and abilities that will make them great and successful in life, people are born with *potential*. Potential is nurtured or practiced in the environment to create talent. Just because you are tall doesn't mean you are going to be an NBA basketball player. Steve Nash wasn't tall, and odds were against a white kid from Canada becoming an NBA MVP. But he did it. Everyone can achieve world-class performance and mastery in his or her chosen field, be it music, sports, the arts, etc. with a lot of hard work.

We tend to believe that Tiger Woods and Mozart were simply born with the innate ability to excel at golf or musical composition. That is simply not true. Any of us may have been as great in either golf or composing, had we been born to Earl Woods or Leopold Mozart, their mentor fathers. By the age of two, they were in an environment in which this potential could blossom. Neither Tiger nor his father suggested that he was born with a particular gift for golf. When Tiger was in his high chair, he was watching his father practice his own golf swing. Tiger has said, "Golf for me was an apparent attempt to emulate the person I looked up to more than anyone, my father." Asked to explain Tiger's phenomenal success, father and son always gave the same reason: hard work.

I've created a little formula to remember this by:

TALENT = ENVIRONMENT(EXPOSURE) + HARD WORK(PRACTICE)

A further secret of masters not covered in the previous chapter is the notion of **deliberate practice**. What this means is that their practice is not willy-nilly and without an objective, but is focused and with purpose. There are eight key features about deliberate practice that have been outlined by researchers.

1. Deliberate practice is highly demanding mentally, requiring high levels of focus and concentration. You must get in the "zone" for it to be effective.

2. It is designed to specifically improve performance—to strengthen it beyond its current levels.

3. It must continue for long periods of time. (Back to the 10,000 hour rule).

4. It must be repeated.

5. It requires continuous feedback on results. This is where having a great teacher or coach can be invaluable.

6. Pre-performance preparation is essential. This is where goal setting comes in.

7. It involves self-observation and self-reflection. This is where you are checking in on how you are doing it as you are doing it.

8. It involves careful reflection on performance after practice sessions are completed. This is where you check in to how you are progressing related to your vision or goals.

For example, just jamming on the piano is not deliberate practice. Practicing the song with a metronome without the sheet music and playing it perfectly 3 times in a row with no mistakes, continually observing results and making adjustments, and doing that for hours every day—that's deliberate practice.

The end result of deliberate practice is what most people call "talent."

If you say you don't have the genes or the talent, what you are really saying is that you have been lazy, inconsistent, and undetermined in your pursuits and don't know where you want to go.

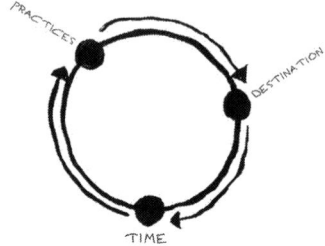

5 MASTERS/KINGS AND THEIR SECRETS

"At the heart of it, mastery is practice. Mastery is staying on the path."

George Leonard

Studying masters and what they did to arrive at their destinations is an important part of becoming a master yourself. What did these people practice? What did they do every day? Success leaves clues. Below are some examples.

Tiger Woods

"When Tiger Woods was an infant, his dad, Earl, moved his high chair into the garage. This was where Earl practiced his golf swing, hitting balls into a soccer net after work. Tiger was captivated by the swift movement. For hours on end, he would watch his father smack hundreds of balls. When Tiger was nine months old, Earl sawed off the top of an old golf club. Tiger could barely walk – and he had yet to utter a single word – but he quickly began teeing off on the Astroturf next to his father. When Tiger was 18 months old, Earl started taking him to the driving range. By the age of three, Tiger was playing nine hole courses, and shooting a 48. That same year, he began identifying the swing flaws of players on the PGA tour. ("Look Daddy," Tiger would say, "that man has a reverse pivot!") He finally beat his father – by a single stroke, with a score of 71 – when he was eleven. At fifteen, he became the youngest player to ever win the United States Junior Amateur championship. At eighteen, he became the youngest player to ever win the United States Amateur championship, a title he kept for the next three years. In 1997, when he was only 21, Tiger won the Masters at Augusta by the largest margin in a major championship in the 20th century. Two months later he became the number one golfer in the world." *(Excerpt from Jonah Lehrer in an article on Wired.com)*

Now Tiger may be a master in golf, but we can see how his practices are in other areas of his life—like relationships, aren't at the same level. So the lesson from Tiger is one of balance. Being a virtuoso could still mean that you are unconscious in other areas of your life. It's important to look at all the areas of your life.

Stephen King

Stephen King has been dedicated to his craft from an early age, continuing to write when times were tough. He worked as a laborer in a mill as well as in a laundry earning $1.50 per hour to support his family. He taught high school English classes and wrote on the evenings and weekends. He sent short stories off to men's magazines for publications, and would earn a few hundred dollars here and there. In his memoir *On Writing*, he shared: "I wrote my first two novels, *Carrie* and *'Salem's Lot* in the laundry room of a doublewide trailer, pounding away on my wife's portable Olivetti typewriter and balancing a child's desk on my thighs."

Imagine this day in 1973. He's been earning dollars per day just getting by, and he gets a phone call from his publisher about a manuscript he had since forgotten about -- *Carrie*. You may know this book from it's movie adaptation. His publisher asks him if he is sitting down. He says the paperback rights have been sold for four hundred thousand dollars. That would be like a million in today's dollars. He literally could not believe his ears.

His life changed, but he stayed dedicated to his craft, to the practice of writing. He could have just stopped right there. But he kept at it. He has published over 50 books, with some being turned into movie classics such as "The Running Man", "Misery", and "The Shining" with Jack Nicholson.

His writing schedule is clear-cut. He writes in the mornings, and when he is working on a project he does not stop and does not slow down unless he has to. He will write every day, including Christmas, the Fourth, and his birthday if he's on a project. He will write ten pages, or 2,000 words a day, and only under dire circumstances does he allow himself to shut down before he gets to his 2,000 word daily goal. He clearly has focus. But on the other hand, he remains balanced. When he's not writing, he's not working at all, although during these times he gets antsy.

He knows the value of sticking to his practices and never giving up in the quest for mastery. He wrote: "...stopping a piece of work just because it's hard, either emotionally or imaginatively, is a bad idea. Sometimes you have to go on when you don't feel like it, and sometimes you're doing good work when it feels like all you're managing is to shovel shit from a sitting position." And he also speaks about the time it takes to create good writing: "...it's also the result of the thousands of hours that writer has spent composing, and the *tens* of thousands of hours he/she may have spent reading the compositions of others."

Oprah Winfrey

Most people know Oprah as one of the most iconic faces on TV as well as one of the richest and most successful women in the world. Oprah faced a hard road to get to that position, however, enduring a rough and often abusive childhood as well as numerous career setbacks including being fired from her job as a television reporter because she was "unfit for TV." She has dedicated her life to her work, running her show and a magazine concurrently, along with numerous outside projects like building a school for girls in South Africa.

After 25 years and 5,000 shows, she has definitely put in the 10,000 hours of mastery into her work. She has said, "Do the one thing you think you cannot do. Fail at it. Try again. Do better the second time. The only people who never tumble are those who never mount the high wire. This is your moment. Own it." She maintains a daily practice of journaling, quiet reflection and meditation, and reading from spiritual texts.

Oprah too has had her struggles in her health practices, publicly see-sawing in weight. She has openly admitted to a food addiction, stating, "My drug of choice is food. I use food for the same reasons an addict uses drugs: to comfort, to soothe, to ease stress." Oprah's life teaches the value of sticking to something, and everyone has struggles no matter how wealthy or powerful. We are all growing. There's always room for evolution.

Kris Carr

In 2003, 31-year-old actress/photographer Kris Carr was diagnosed with a rare and incurable cancer. Weeks later she began filming her story for her inspirational and highly recommended documentary called *Crazy Sexy Cancer*. Taking a seemingly tragic situation and turning it into a creative expression, Kris shared her inspirational story of survival with courage, strength, and lots of humor.

With experimental treatment as her only option, Kris became determined to find answers where there were none. She sold everything and hit the road, traveling throughout the country interviewing experts in alternative medicine as she tenaciously dove head first into a fascinating and often hilarious holistic world.

Completely transforming her formerly old practices to new ones, she gave up her old diet and began juicing every day. Years later her cancer is now in remission without chemotherapy or radiation. She has written 3 bestselling books and has become an inspiring leader for the health and wellness revolution.

Michael Phelps

The American swimmer, Michael Phelps, leaves behind his legacy as the most decorated and greatest Olympian of all time with an overall sum of 22 medals. He won six gold and two bronze medals at Athens in 2004, eight gold medals in Beijing in 2008, and four gold and two silver medals at the London Olympics in 2012.

Michael began swimming at the age of 7, partly because of the influence of his sisters and partly as an outlet for his high energy. By the age of 10, he held a record for his age group and began to be coached by Bob Bowman. Bowman believed that the key to success was creating the right routines. He created for Michael the right mental routines to practice before and after races, he crafted his diet and practice schedules, and stretching and sleep routines.

In a given week of training, Michael swam 50 miles, and consumed 6,000 calories or more per day. He trained every day, including Sundays, figuring it gave him 52 more training days per year than his competitors. He had been practicing for over 20 years at being the best in the world when he retired in 2012. His record of 18 Olympic gold medals may never be matched.

Phelps exemplifies dedication, perseverance, and plain old hard work. He has become a master in one area, now the real question is how is he in the other areas of his life.

George Leonard

George Leonard, a pioneer in the field of human potentialities, is author of twelve books, including *The Transformation, Education and Ecstasy, The Silent Pulse, The Ultimate Athlete, and Mastery.*

Leonard holds a fifth-degree black belt in aikido and is co-founder of a martial arts school. Over the course of 34 years there was rarely a day in which he missed practicing his art. He is founder of Leonard Energy Training (LET), a transformative practice inspired by aikido, which he has introduced to some 50,000 people in the U.S. and abroad.

Madonna

This pop and beauty icon has been in the public eye since her debut hit in the 80's. Now in her 50's, she manages her health strictly. She has followed a macrobiotic diet for years, eating whole grains, sea vegetables, beans, soups, teas, and some fish. She avoids all sweets, meat, and cheese. Some macrobiotic dieters also chew their food 50 times, never cook with electricity or microwaves, and adjust their food choices based on season, climate, and other factors.

Madonna has been a devotee of an extremely challenging form of yoga, called Ashtanga Yoga, for years, practicing up to two hours a day, six days a week. She also practices pilates and goes horse riding regularly. She follows Ayurvedic medicine, a 5,000 year old practice from India which utilizes herbs, diet, and massage to harmonize the body.

Madonna has also been of service, creating the Raising Malawi foundation which works to help children orphaned from AIDS. She runs a school for girls, and adopted two children from the poverty-stricken country.

Deepak Chopra

World-renowned doctor, author, speaker, and alternative medicine expert Deepak Chopra has a daily regimen as follows. He meditates early in the morning from 4 to 6am. He then spends the next hour and a half either in the gym or walking. He carries various devices that monitor his sleep and exercise patterns so he can track his progress over time. He follows Ayurvedic practices and a well balanced diet.

Although he has an amazingly busy schedule he remains in the present. His assistant emails his schedule for the day, the night before, and he doesn't look at it until *after* his morning practices. He stays in the present. So if you ask him what he is doing tomorrow, he will say he will be up at the break of dawn for his practices, and then he will be of service wherever life calls him.

He does a shorter evening meditation, and then before he goes to bed he does quiet reflection on his day; how he wishes to see his world, and what role he can play in the future.

Robin Sharma

Canadian author and motivational speaker Robin Sharma follows the following success practices. I highly recommend his book *The Monk Who Sold his Ferrari*.

- ✓ up between 4 and 5 am five times a week
- ✓ a 60 minute Holy Hour once he's up to work on his mind, body, heart and spirit. He also plans, dreams and thinks here
- ✓ 5 big-time workouts a week
- ✓ a 90 minute massage every 7 days
- ✓ a world-class diet (1-2 desserts every week—life isn't meant to be too strict)
- ✓ a period of journaling most days
- ✓ a period of reading each day (from Harvard Business Review to Dwell)
- ✓ affirmations throughout the day—especially in the shower
- ✓ a weekly planning session (He also reviews his goals here; usually Sunday mornings)
- ✓ at least one conversation with an interesting person each week to keep his passion high and to surround him with big ideas

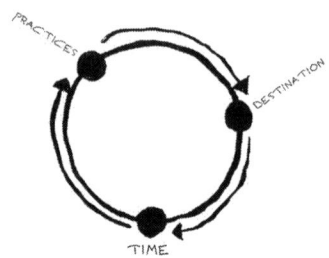

6 IT'S JUST A MATTER OF TIME

Everyone wants things instantaneously. Instant gratification. Fast and easy. But it's the long journey that makes us who we are. Focus on this step right now, and don't try to rush the process. This isn't a race.

As a child, I loved reading Aesop's fables. We've all heard this story.

Rabbit and Turtle

One day a rabbit was boasting about how fast he could run. He was laughing at the turtle for being so slow. Much to the rabbit's surprise, the turtle challenged him to a race. The rabbit thought this was a good joke and accepted the challenge. The fox was to be the umpire of the race. As the race began, the rabbit raced way ahead of the turtle, just like everyone thought. The rabbit got to the halfway point and could not see the turtle anywhere. He was hot and tired and decided to stop and take a short nap.

Even if the turtle passed him, he would be able to race to the finish line ahead of him. All this time the turtle kept walking step by step by step. He never quit no matter how hot or tired he got. He just kept going. However, the rabbit slept longer than he had thought and woke up. He could not see the turtle anywhere! He went at full-speed to the finish line but found the turtle there waiting for him.

Patience, persistence, perseverance. These are the qualities that determine success in life. I always tell my mentoring clients to be the turtle in life. To be okay with the process, and to be okay with things taking time. I recently learned a Beethoven sonata on the piano. It took me an entire *year* practicing to perfect the song.

Picasso

There is a story of Pablo Picasso, sitting in a quiet sidewalk café. He was approached by a woman who had recognized him as the world renowned painter. She immediately approached him and asked if he would draw her something, anything that she could show off to her friends. Picasso obliged. He took a napkin and drew a quick pencil sketch. As he handed it to the woman, he said: "that will be $100,000."

The woman was astounded. "$100,000, that is ridiculous! It only took you thirty seconds to draw that."

Picasso replied, "Miss, it took me thirty years to do that masterpiece in thirty seconds."

When it comes to practice, we've got to put in the time. There's no way around it.

"We must suffer from one of two pains: the pain of discipline or the pain of regret. The difference is discipline weighs ounces, while regret weighs tons."

Jim Rohn

It's practice now, or pay the price later. Take care of your health now, or wind up in the hospital later. Manage your finances now, or end up broke later. Work on your relationship now, or end up alone later. One way is proactive, the other is reactive. One is conscious, the other unconscious. Every moment we are practicing our destination.

Here's the big irony.

Easy life now, hard later.

Hard now, easy later.

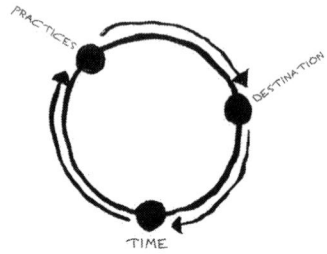

7 CHECK YOURSELF

"You better check yo self before you wreck yo self."
Ice Cube, rapper

The greater the distance to our destination, the more we have to check our practice to make sure we are on the right path.

Imagine you are on a putting green. If you are two inches from the hole, if your putter is a few degrees off, it will still go into the hole. But if you are 500 yards away and you swing your driver and it is a few degrees off center, you will be totally off the golf course!

If the distance to your destination was the moon, a few degrees off would mean a million miles off course.

CHECK YOURSELF

Check in daily to see whether you are still on the right track or not with your practices.

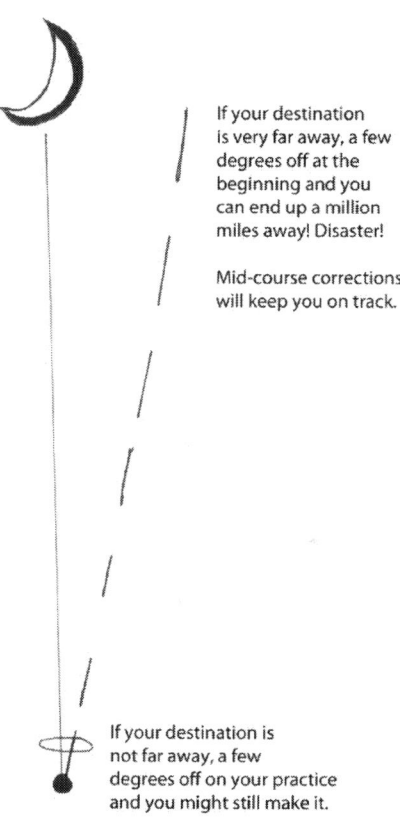

If your destination is very far away, a few degrees off at the beginning and you can end up a million miles away! Disaster!

Mid-course corrections will keep you on track.

If your destination is not far away, a few degrees off on your practice and you might still make it.

My partner tells a story from his early twenties when he was on a road trip. He was driving from Lake Tahoe to Vail, Colorado, which was going to take longer than a day. He drove across Nevada on deserted highway 50 and it was getting late. Driving along jamming to good music, he made a turn and got on the wrong highway. It was an hour and a half before he realized he was on the wrong road. There was a sign giving the distance to Salt Lake City, and he wanted to be heading towards Denver! He turned right around, but he lost 3 hours of time before getting on the right path. How could someone not know they were on the wrong highway? They weren't paying attention!

If we've been going down the wrong path for a while with the wrong practices, it can take a while before we get back, heading down the right path. For instance, if you've been practicing poverty by going into debt, it can take some time before you pay down your debts and get yourself back to zero. Then you can start to build up a nest egg for saving and investing.

Before you go too far down a path, check the signs! Are you ignoring any signals right now? Life is always trying to get a hold of us, it's just a question of whether or not we are listening. There are signposts along the way, and we might be ignoring them. An example of this is taking prescription medication for acid reflux, without changing your diet. You continue down the wrong highway eating poorly, suppressing symptoms and eventually leading to a major illness, just like ending up in Salt Lake City instead of Vail.

CHECK YOURSELF

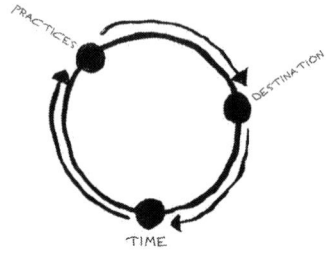

8 EVERY PRACTICE MATTERS

Formula for SUCCESS = a few simple practices every day

Fomula for FAILURE = the result/destination of a few errors in judgment practiced every day

Now why would someone repeat the wrong practice every day?

Because they don't think it matters.

If they haven't read a book in 90 days, this lack of discipline does not seem to have any immediate impact on their life.

Eating the wrong foods, smoking, drinking… people go on making the same decisions because they think it doesn't matter. They don't realize they are committing a slow and gradual suicide.

The pain and regret of these simple practices, simple errors in judgment, have only been delayed for a future time.

In the short term, these practices don't seem to make a difference. People just drift from one day to the next, repeating the same wrong practices.

Failure's most dangerous attribute is its subtlety.

There is this "seduction of gradualism" that lulls us into a comfortable numbness, unaware that Niagara Falls is at the end of this happy calm stream.

Our health deteriorates so slowly that we don't notice until something serious happens and we wind up in the hospital with cancer. We have a crisis of illness and then recover, but our recovery will not be the same level we started at. This is our new level of health that we get used to. We then build up more toxic accumulation until our next crisis. We recover, and sink to an even lower baseline of everyday health, and so on and so on. The same process could be said to take place for sinking into debt, or drifting apart in our relationship.

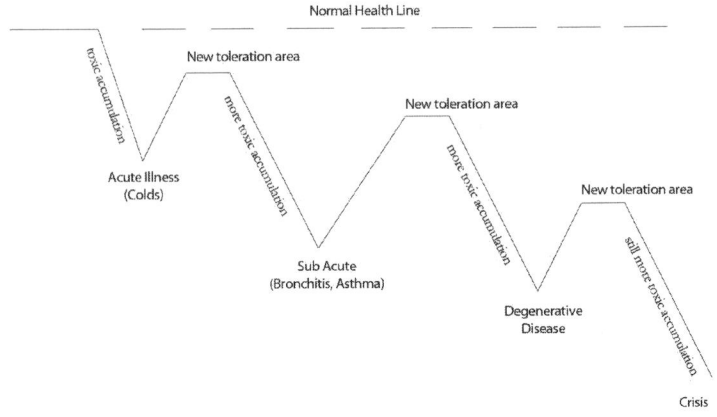

If you drop a frog in a pot of boiling water, it will of course frantically try to clamber out. But if you place it gently in a pot of tepid water and turn the heat on low, it will float there quite placidly. As the water gradually heats up, the frog will sink into a tranquil stupor, exactly like one of us in a hot bath, and before long, with a smile on its face, it will unresistingly allow itself to be boiled to death.

Version of the story from Daniel Quinn's The Story of B

We can very easily become like the frog in this story if we aren't conscious of what we are practicing every day. So take an inventory of your daily practices and see if you are living in gradually boiling water. **Every practice matters.** Over time, everything becomes transparent.

CHECK YOURSELF

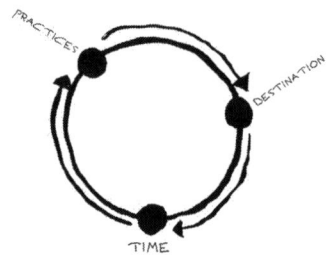

9 SPIRITUAL PRACTICE

THE PRACTICES OF SPIRIT

1. Put your inner world first
2. Gratitude
3. Connect to nature, intuition, animals
4. Read inspirational texts
5. Creativity
6. Faith

SPIRITUAL PRACTICE

> **Practice is the seed bed of miracles.**
> *Michael Murphy*

Put your inner world first

Spiritual masters know that the outer world is created from the inner world. They have their priorities in order, and put connecting to their inner world first. This shows up by having time spent each day in meditation, quiet reading, reflection, and contemplation. They do this first thing upon rising in the morning because they know that the quality of their day depends on the quality of their connection to Source.

> **"Nowhere can man find a quieter or more untroubled retreat than in his own soul."**
> *Marcus Aurelius*

I love Eckhart Tolle's work, and the passage below is from his excellent book, *The Power of Now*. He sums up the message of this book in an eloquent way. I have been speaking throughout this book about "outer purpose", but there is a greater purpose to your life, and that is your "inner purpose."

THE INNER PURPOSE OF YOUR LIFE'S JOURNEY

"When you are on a journey, it is certainly helpful to know where you are going or at least the general direction in which you are moving, but don't forget: the only thing that is ultimately real about your journey is the step that you are taking at this moment. That's all there ever is.

Your life's journey has an outer purpose and an inner purpose. The outer purpose is to arrive at your goal or destination, to accomplish what you set out to do, to achieve this or that, which of course, implies future. But if your destination, or the steps you are going to take in the future, take up so much of your attention that they become more important to you than the step you are taking now, then you completely miss the journey's inner purpose, which has nothing to do with *where* you are going or *what* you are doing, but everything to do with *how*. It has nothing to do with future but everything to do with the quality of your consciousness at this moment. The outer purpose belongs to the horizontal dimension of space and time; the inner purpose concerns a deepening of your Being in the vertical dimensions of the timeless Now. Your outer journey may contain a million steps; your inner journey only has one: the step you are taking right now. As you become more deeply aware of this one step, you realize that it already contains within itself all the other steps as well as the destination. This one step then becomes transformed into an expression of perfection, an act of great beauty and quality. It will have taken you into the Being, and the light of Being will shine through it. This is both the purpose and the fulfillment of your inner journey, the journey into yourself."

Take a moment now to contemplate what he just said. You might even close the book for a moment and close your eyes, or even reread the passage.

Ultimately, arriving at our destination creates contentment, but cannot create lasting fulfillment because nothing ever lasts, and everything is constantly changing. All we have is this moment right now and who we are being. So what we do in this moment right now, and how we do it is the most important thing there is.

The inner purpose is to awaken, the outer purpose is to arrive at your destination. The practice of learning music is that you are fully present and awake in this moment, learning this one measure. Every practice—health, wealth, relationship—becomes a meditative spiritual practice of awakening.

Gratitude

"If the only prayer you said in your whole life was, "thank you," that would suffice."
Meister Eckhart

"God gave you a gift of 86,400 seconds today. Have you used one to say 'thank you?'"
William A. Ward

"The only people with whom you should try to get even are those who have helped you."
John E. Southard

A great way to get yourself connected to your inner world is to give thanks for all that you have. One practice I recommend is to keep a Gratitude Journal. In it you write down all the things you are thankful for. You can do this daily, and it is a wonderful way to keep yourself centered and focused on what is important.

Another great spiritual practice of gratitude is to be of service to others. This can manifest in many ways, whether it is donating your time to a cause, or simply being of service in your vocation, whatever it may be.

Connect to nature, intuition, animals

I have always had a love of nature and animals. Growing up on the farm I was surrounded by natural beauty and by lots of animals. I once had a cat named Tigger that used to follow me around everywhere I went. I raised her from the time she was a kitten and I loved her so much. We also had a baby calf that would follow me everywhere. Today, I have two dogs that I connect to daily, and it is one of the things I cherish most in my life. They sit by my side every morning while I am reading, journaling, and contemplating. Animals are in such a state of present moment awareness that just being around them puts you in a more conscious state.

If you don't have animals, spending time in nature also puts you back in connection with Source. In the quiet and stillness of nature we see that we are one with everything, and move from our heads to our hearts where our inner wisdom resides. Medicine men of many cultures say that plants and nature speak to them. We have lost this capacity due to the loudness of thoughts going on in our minds, but regular forays into nature can help you still the mind and hear the wisdom nature has to offer.

Many of us have had moments where we felt that something was not right, as if it was a warning. This happens to me frequently, and I have learned to pay attention when I get a signal. I'm sure we've all had moments where we did not listen to that inner voice and "trust our vibes", and something bad happened that we could have avoided. The practice of listening to your intuition and trusting it is an important one. It takes moving from the mental chattering mind down into the heart and the body to be sensitive to it. Practicing yoga and meditation can bring you into your body and more receptive to your intuition.

> **"As long as you do not live totally in the body, you do not live totally in the Self."**
>
> *B. K. S. Iyengar*

Read inspirational texts

Every morning along with my reading from various subjects, I always take time to read from the great spiritual texts that I cherish. I especially love reading from the Tao Te Ching. Even just reading one passage, closing the book and sitting in silent contemplation of that one passage is enough. Many times I will read something I had read before, but that day for some reason a new understanding I hadn't seen before will come to my awareness. I will usually then write about it in my journal. But it never fails that I get "ah-ha's" from the same books at a later time.

Creativity

I have found in my own life that creativity is a spiritual practice. In the act of creation, whether we are drawing, painting, writing, making music, and so on, we connect to the ultimate creativity of the universe, and it flows through us. We move out of the way, lose sense of ourselves and our story, and become one with the practice. We move into "flow", which is a heightened state of consciousness we are all capable of, and one in which we are directly tapped into universal intelligence. We become an instrument whereby the song of the universe can be played through us.

I also know that creativity is a healing path. In my early twenties, I went through a healing period where I painted my way back to my heart. I had stored a lot of repressed feelings, and I found that painting could express how I really felt when words fell short. At this time, I began leading creativity groups that utilized spontaneous singing, dancing, writing, and drawing. Through being in the moment, I got to witness the healing effect of how creativity can transform darkness into light.

Faith

"Once a man was about to cross the sea. A wise man tied a leaf in a corner of his robe and said to him: "Don't be afraid. Have faith and walk on the water. But look here—the moment you lose faith You will drown."

Sri Ramakrishna

The lesson in the story above can be found in the leaf the wise man tied to the robe. The man was to remember leaves on his journey. We've all seen leaves in autumn fall on water. What happens? Fallen leaves float because they have surrendered. When we become still and open ourselves rather than curl up tightly, we are supported and carried by the invisible sea that supports all life. And just as fish can't see the ocean they swim in, we can't see the spirit that sustains us.

A WORD ABOUT SPIRITUALITY

I have a very grounded approach to spirituality. It can be easy to get seduced into the "airy fairy" world of gurus and spiritual leaders. Ultimately for me, spirituality is how we do everything. What we are demonstrating in this moment is what I call my "Spirituality BS Detector." And it works like this.

I ask the following questions:

How are you with your money?

How are you in your relationships?

How is your health?

What have you done with your "talents" (gifts from Source)?

So even though a person may tout their "spirituality", how they are here on Earth now and every day is a greater indicator of spirituality than anything they could ever say. I have come across numerous "religious" or "spiritual" individuals who spouted or parroted some beautiful and provocative words that seduced many, and were later discovered to be embezzling money, sleeping with followers, or were grossly overweight. How many priests who were practicing daily in their religion and giving sermons to congregations were secretly pedophiles, lusting after young children? As Emerson said, "Who you are speaks so loudly I can't hear what you're saying."

In my opinion, these people are not using their "talents" and just as in the parable from the Bible, they will all be taken away. The story is below in case you aren't familiar with it.

> A man who is preparing to leave on a journey entrusts his possessions to his servants. He distributes his wealth among three servants, apportioned to them on the basis of their abilities. To the first he entrusted five talents, to the second two talents, and to the third one talent. The first two servants quickly set to work with their master's money. The third servant did not invest his master's

money at all; he dug a hole in the ground and buried his master's money. When the master returned, the first two eagerly met their master, apparently delighted in the opportunity to multiply their master's money. Both were commended as "good and faithful servants"; both were rewarded with increased responsibilities in their master's service; both were invited to share in their master's joy.

The master's dealings with the third servant is a very different matter. This servant came to his master with only the talent his master had originally entrusted to him. He did not increase his master's money at all. In fact, if this were to take place today, that money would likely be worth less, due to inflation. This servant offered a feeble excuse for his conduct. He told his master that he was a harsh and cruel man, a man who was demanding, and who expected gain where he had not labored. He contended that this is why he was afraid to take a risk with any kind of investment. And so he simply hid the money, and now he returned it, without any gain. The master rebuked this slave for being evil and lazy. He took his talent from him, gave it to the one who earned ten, and cast this fellow into outer darkness, where there was weeping and gnashing of teeth.

So you could interpret this story in many ways, but the way I interpret it here is that by not using your god-given gifts in life you are in effect "burying them", and not sharing them with the world. You are wasting your precious time by not practicing and using your mind, body, and spirit to improve your condition and that of those around you, and therefore you are destined to lose it all.

If you don't take care of your health, it will be taken from you.

If you don't take care of your money, it will be taken from you.

If you don't take care of your relationship, it will be taken from you.

HOW WE CHANGE THE WORLD

**If there is light in the soul,
There will be beauty in the person.
If there is beauty in the person,
There will be harmony in the house.
If there is harmony in the house,
There will be order in the nation.
If there is order in the nation,
There will be peace in the world.**

Chinese Proverb

As you can see in the saying above, through a series of linkages our inner light changes the entire world. And our inner light is directly affected by our daily practices. Our practices have the ability to affect the whole world. As we practice the right things, our inner flame begins to brighten and grow. This is how we make a difference in the world.

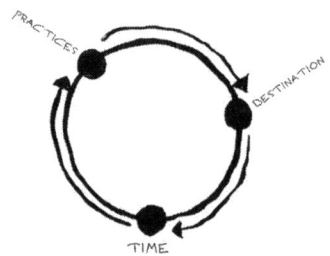

10 ULTIMATE PRACTICE

"Sow a thought and you reap an action; sow an act and you reap a habit; sow a habit and you reap a character; sow a character and you reap a destiny."
Ralph Waldo Emerson

Most tend to think that once they HAVE money, they will DO what they love, and they will BE happy. The truth is they have it backwards.

The way it should be is when I am BEING what I intend, I am DOING what I set out to do, and I am HAVING the experience of happiness in that moment. Happiness is a journey, and it is in the being and doing part that we experience joy. It is not some future event, it is only in the now that we experience it.

In the act of practice, you are actually BEing in that moment what you set out to be. So if you are practicing piano, in that moment you are a pianist. If you are running preparing for a race, in that act you have become a runner. When you save 10¢ out of a dollar, you are being wealthy.

And during that act of practice you are literally re-creating yourself, that very moment into a whole new being.

The latest findings in neuroscience support this conclusion. Scientists used to believe the brain was fixed once you reached adulthood. But recent studies have shown that new neural connections are being created when you learn new things and take on new practices. It is known as "neuroplasticity."

This is great news, because you are not a victim any more, you are empowered to become whatever you set out to be. As we have shown in this book, it all comes down to what you practice every day.

Right now are you:

Being healthy	OR	Being sick
Being wealthy	OR	Being poor
Being connected	OR	Being isolated
Being great	OR	Being mediocre

"The primary mechanism to acquire new habits by the subconscious mind after the age of six is through the use of repetitive behaviors, and hence the need for 'practice.' Evolution, like heaven… is not a destination, but a practice…"

Bruce Lipton, developmental biologist and author

You BECOME what you PRACTICE. You are in a constant evolution throughout your life, and by practicing, you are fulfilling your innate drive to evolve and grow, to become great, like the infinite intelligence of nature.

You might be saying, "That's great, but I've tried to give up smoking (or some other negative practice), and I just can't seem to kick it." Well, here's how you do it. We only change out of inspiration or desperation.

HOW TO CREATE NEW PRACTICES

"In reality, the subconscious is an emotionless database of stored programs, whose function is strictly concerned with reading environmental signals and engaging in hardwired behavioral programs, no questions asked, no judgments made. The subconscious mind is a programmable 'hard drive' into which our life experiences are downloaded."

Bruce Lipton

First, understand that practices are programmed in the subconscious mind. There are brain circuits wired together for specific practices, created through repetition or routine. So when you take on new practices, you are creating new circuits in your brain, like a programmer writing new software to run in an operating system.

Practices are triggered to play when they are set off by a "cue" in the environment, just like a program is set off by a specific action, like hitting "Enter", or typing in a command on the keyboard. Triggers for practices include:

1) Location—for example, whenever you pass by the Starbucks on the way to work, you feel compelled to get a white chocolate mocha with extra whipped cream;

2) Time—for example, every morning when you wake up, you have a cigarette;

3) Emotional state—for example, when you get angry at your partner you automatically shut down and go in the other room;

4) Other people—for example, when your ex calls, you go and eat a box of cookies; and

5) Preceding action—for example, whenever you drink alcohol, then you light up a cigarette.

Every practice is linked to a good feeling. You get a momentary payoff after the action, and over time you get a long term result, or destination. For example, when a problem arises and you feel anxious, you light up a cigarette as an automatic practice, which is linked to the good feeling of being in control and being relaxed. But long term, you know where that leads.

The first key is to understand the triggers for your behavior, and the reward or payoff it is linked to. Once you understand this loop, you simply substitute a new practice in place of the automatic behavior. It requires you to become conscious, which is the "King" in our story from Chapter 1. Each time the trigger happens, the King must step in, and direct the new practice.

You are then literally creating new neural pathways in your brain that strengthen each time you do your new practice. You are creating yourself anew. As you do so, you begin to train your inner muscle called "willpower." Studies over the last decade have shown that literally, willpower is like a muscle that gets stronger when used.

Studies have also shown that when people strengthened their willpower muscles in one part of their lives—in the gym or a money management program—that strength spilled over into what they ate or how hard they worked. Once willpower became stronger, it touched everything.

Speaking of willpower, what drives me to do a practice is that higher power, "Thy Will", Spirit, Source, Intelligence, or whatever you want to call it. This is what the King within you taps into and has the Servant carry out. "Thy will" is from your higher nature. Strengthening your willpower through practice is evolving you to your higher self. It's not what you get at the end, it's who you become along the way. It's how we humans evolve, and it's what separates us from our animal nature.

THE POWER OF PRACTICE

So back to our King and Servant story. When you start to create new practices, you become stronger like the King. As the new practices take hold, they spread throughout your entire kingdom. You are the ruler of your domain. The King is the conscious driver, who knows the destination.

Never before has the world needed more Kings, masters of their lives to rule over their Servant natures. There is havoc, anxiety, disharmony, disease, disconnect, and self indulgence. Only when we practice our way to mastery and evolve as humans to demonstrate our highest visions can we arrive at the throne of our existence and become true stewards of our lives.

The only thing standing between our present conditions and our greatest lives is our practices. Yes, they will require a decision, a determination, patience, and some discomfort, but this initial resistance turns into a deep contentment in the long run.

Sharing our talent, revitalizing our bodies, restoring our souls, enriching our relationships, building financial freedom is ultimately the practice of love… love for our lives, love for our gifts, and love for each other.

The right practices over time bestow countless blessings. It is who we become by showing up every day and doing the work that ultimately matters. We become the King and the kingdom flourishes. There is harmony and abundance.

It does seem paradoxical, that hard work now leads to an easy life later, and easy life now leads to a hard life later. But as these practices require sacrifices now, they restore us later. They open us to becoming a whole new person. We exchange our momentary pleasure practices to strength, willpower, and beauty.

This effort eventually becomes effortless.

Even though it might be hard to start, eventually it can't be stopped…

In a culture intoxicated with the promises of the quick fix, it is the long term practices that change a person.

Whether you are learning the piano, or learning to be a more compassionate person, it is our practices over time that lead us from Servant to King, from being reactive to being proactive.

We all possess a vast, untapped potential to learn, to grow, to love, to feel deeply, to create beyond imaginings, and there are few tragedies so pervasive as the waste of that potential.

I believe that everybody has the potential to be great in all areas of life, and to be able to create those practices that lead you to your greatest life. The key to the kingdom is now in your hand.

Decide where you really want to go and take that one step, learn that one measure, pay yourself that one dollar, do the one loving act of kindness, and today practice your way to your ultimate destination.

So what are you waiting for?

1) Pick a DESTINATION. Really define it in concrete terms. Write out the steps for how you are going to get there. Write out how you plan to overcome potential obstacles, stresses, or resistance that might stand in your way.

2) Create your PRACTICES. Find a teacher, coach, or mentor. Study the greats to find out how to get there. Adopt their practices, and do them correctly. What steps did they take?

3) Fill your TIME with repetitive and deliberate PRACTICES. Begin today with one step. Check in regularly to make sure you are still on track.

4) BECOME what you have set out to be.

In 10,000 hours I'll see you there!

You were born with potential

You were born with goodness and trust

You were born with ideals and dreams

You were born with greatness

You were born with wings

You are not meant for crawling, so don't

You have wings

Learn to use them and fly!

Rumi

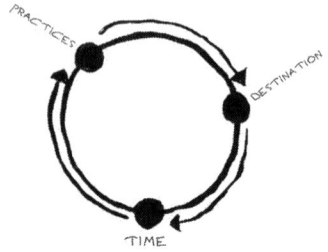

AFTERWORD: AS YOU PRACTICE

"As a man thinketh in his heart [and practices], so is he."
Proverbs 23:7 [with my addition]

Some of you readers may have read the book *As A Man Thinketh* by James Allen. It is one of the all time great books on the power of the subconscious mind and on positive thinking. It greatly influenced "The Secret."

My take on the quote and on "The Secret", as you can see above is that it is what you **practice** that you become and what you create in your life. Thinking is important, but it's where the rubber meets the road in your practices that makes all the difference. I haven't found any texts that really address this.

AFTERWORD: AS YOU PRACTICE

What I have done below is revised some of the text of James Allen's work and added in the word practice and destination in **bold** to his original words, and you can see that the insertions still make sense and make an even stronger point. Enjoy this new take on an all-time classic work.

Thought **Practice** and Character

"As we think in our hearts and then **practice** with our body so are we". We are literally *what we think* and what we **practice** every day, our character being the complete sum of all our **practices**.

Practice is the blossom of thought and is the fruit that ends up on our tree. We will gather the sweet and bitter fruits of our own planting.

What we are was designed and built by our own thoughts and **practices**. If our **practices** are healthy and beneficial, joy will follow us as surely as our shadows follow us on a sunny day.

Cause and effect is as absolute and undeviating as it is in the hidden realm of thought as in the world of visible **practice.**

A noble character is not a thing of favor or chance but is the natural result of continued effort of right **practice**.

We are made or unmade by ourselves. In the armory of thoughts and **practices** we forge the weapons we use to destroy ourselves, and we also fashion the tools we use to build for ourselves the greatest paradise.

By the right choices and the true applications of our **practices,** we ascend to divine perfection; by the abuses and wrong **practices**, we descend to the lowest levels of existence. Between these two extremes are all grades of character, and we are their makers and masters.

You are the master of your thought and also the master of your everyday **practices**, the molder of your character and the maker and shaper of your condition, environment, and destiny.

As a being of power, intelligence, and love, and the lord of your own **practices**, you hold the key to every situation and contain within yourself that transforming and regenerative agency by which you may make yourself what you will.

You are always the master, even in your weakest and most abandoned state; but in your weakness and degradation you are the foolish master who misgoverns your household by practicing everyday the wrong **practices**.

When you begin to reflect upon your condition and search for how you got to where you are, then you become the wise master, directing your energies with intelligence, and fashioning your thoughts and **practices** to fruitful issues.

Such is the *conscious* master, and only you can become a conscious master by discovering *within yourself* the laws of **practice**. This discovery is totally a matter of application, self-analysis and experience.

Only by much searching and mining are gold and diamonds obtained, and you can find every truth connected with your being, if you will dig deep into the mine of your life and discover the simple **practices** that will take you to the destination of your choice.

AFTERWORD: AS YOU PRACTICE

The fact that you are the maker of your character, the molder of your life, and the builder of your destiny, you may prove, if you will watch, decide, and do the **practices**, you will see the effects upon yourself, upon others, and upon your life and circumstances, linking cause and effect by patient **practice** and investigation--even the most trivial, everyday occurrence--as a means of obtaining that knowledge of yourself that leads to understanding, wisdom and power.

It is the law absolute that "Those that seek shall find: to those that know the door shall be opened," for only by patience, ceaseless importunity, and ceaseless **practice** can you enter the door of the temple of wisdom and mastery.

The Effect of Thought and Practice on Circumstance

Your mind and your day can be likened to a garden that may be intelligently cultivated or allowed to run wild -- but whether cultivated or neglected, it must, and will, bring forth.

If no useful seeds, thoughts, and **practices** are put into it, then an abundance of useless weed seeds, (the wrong **practices**), will fall therein, and will continue to produce their kind.

Just as gardeners cultivate their plots, keeping them free from weeds, and growing the flowers and fruits they desire, so may you tend the garden of your life, weeding out all the wrong, useless, and impure thoughts, and cultivating the right **practices** that create the ultimate perfection.

By pursuing this process, you will sooner or later discover that you are the master gardener of your soul, the director of your life.

Thought, **practice**, and character are one, and as character can only manifest and discover itself through environment and circumstance, the outer conditions of your life will always be found to be harmoniously related to your inner state and what you **practice** every day.

This does not mean that your circumstances at any given time are an indication of your *entire* character, but that those circumstances are so intimately connected with some vital thought and **practice**, that for the time being, they are indispensable to your development.

You are where you are by the law of your being; the thoughts and **practices** that you have built into your life have brought you there, and in the arrangement of your life there is no element of chance, but all is the result of a law that cannot err.

As an evolving being, you are where you are in order to learn and to grow, and as you learn the spiritual lesson that any circumstance contains for you, it passes away and gives place to other circumstances.

You are buffeted by circumstances so long as you believe yourself to be a creature affected by outside conditions--but when you realize that you are a creative power, and that you may command the hidden soil and seeds of your being, your thoughts and **practices**, then you become the rightful master of yourself.

All great people who have practiced self-examination and self-discipline know that circumstances grow out of thought and everyday **practices**, for they have noticed that the alterations in their circumstances have been in direct proportion to their altered **practices**.

AFTERWORD: AS YOU PRACTICE

So true is this that when you earnestly apply yourself to remedy the defects in your life, you make swift and marked progress and life begins to change rapidly.

The soul attracts that which it secretly harbors--what it loves, and also what it fears. It reaches the height of its cherished aspirations, and it falls to the depths of its recurring, unexamined fears. Circumstances are the means by which the soul receives its own.

Every thought/practice sown or allowed to fall into one's life and take root there, produces its own, blossoming sooner or later into bearing its own fruits of opportunity and circumstance.

Good thoughts and good **practices** bear good fruit, bad thoughts and bad **practices** bear bad fruit.

The outer world of circumstance shapes itself to the inner world of thought and everyday **practices**, and both pleasant and unpleasant external conditions are the factors that make for the ultimate good of one's life.

As the reaper of your own harvest you learn both by suffering and bliss.

Following the innermost aspirations, and that which you allow yourself to **practice**, you at last arrive at their fruition and fulfillment in the outer conditions of your life. The laws of growth and adjustment apply everywhere.

A person does not just end up in the gutter, overweight, broke, or in a prison by the tyranny of fate or circumstance, but by the path of certain low **practices** and base desires.

Circumstance does not make the person, it reveals the person to himself or herself.

We do not attract what we *want*, we attract what we *are*. Our whims, fancies, and ambitions are thwarted at every step, but our innermost thoughts and **practices** are fed with their own food, be it good or bad.

Our own thoughts and **practices** are the jailers of our fate--they imprison, if they are base; and they are also the angels of freedom--they liberate, if they are noble.

We don't get what we wish and pray for, we get what we justly earn. Our wishes and prayers are only gratified and answered when they harmonize with our everyday **practices**.

In the light of this truth, what then is the meaning of "fighting against circumstances" in our lives? It means that we are continually revolting against an *effect* without, while all the time we are nourishing and **practicing** its cause.

That cause may take the form of a bad **practice**, or an unconscious weakness; but whatever it is, it stubbornly retards the efforts of its possessor, and calls aloud for a remedy.

Most of us are anxious to improve our circumstances, but are unwilling to improve ourselves--and therefore remain bound.

If we do not shrink from honest examination of our thoughts and everyday **practices**, we can never fail to accomplish the object our hearts are set upon.

Even if our sole object is to acquire wealth, we must be prepared to make great personal sacrifices and undertake significant daily **practices** before we can accomplish our object.

AFTERWORD: AS YOU PRACTICE

Here is an example of some rich people who have a painful and persistent disease as the result of gluttony. They are willing to pay large sums of money to get rid of their illness, but they will not sacrifice their **practice** of overeating the wrong foods.

They want to gratify their taste for rich foods in immoderate amounts and have their health as well. Such people are completely unfit for good health, because they have not learned even the first **practice** of a healthy life.

I have introduced this example merely to illustrate the truth that people are the cause -- though nearly always unconsciously -- of their circumstances, and that, while aiming at good ends, they are continually frustrating the accomplishment of those good ends by encouraging thoughts and **practices** that cannot possibly harmonize with those ends.

Good thoughts and **practices** can never produce bad results; bad thoughts and **practices** can never produce good results. Nothing can come from corn but corn, nothing from nettles but nettles.

Suffering is *always* the effect of wrong thought and **practice** in some direction.

It is an indication that we are out of harmony with ourselves, the law of our being. The sole reason for suffering is to purify, to burn out all that is useless or cause change.

The wrong thoughts and **practices** crystalize into habits, which solidify into circumstances of every kind creating adverse conditions; thoughts of fear, doubt, and indecision turn into weak and inconsistent practices, which turn into circumstances of failure, poverty, and dependence; lazy thoughts crystallize into **practices** of uncleanliness and dishonesty, which solidify into circumstances of foulness and poverty; hateful and condemnatory thoughts crystallize into **practices** of accusation and violence, which solidify into circumstances of injury and persecution; selfish thoughts of all kinds crystallize into **practices** that are self-seeking, which solidify into circumstances that are distressing.

On the other hand, beautiful thoughts of all kinds crystallize into **practices** of grace and kindliness, which solidify into genial and sunny circumstances; constructive thoughts crystallize into **practices** of temperance and self-control, which solidify into circumstances of repose and peace; thoughts of courage, self reliance, and decision crystallize into strong and productive **practices**, which solidify into circumstances of success, plenty, and freedom.

We cannot *directly* choose our circumstances, but we can choose our thoughts and our **practices**, and so indirectly, yet surely, shape our circumstances.

Nature works with us and through us to help us gratify the thoughts and **practices** we encourage the most, and opportunities are presented that will most speedily bring to the surface both the good and the destructive patterns.

As soon as we cease from our negative and destructive **practices**, all the world softens towards us, and is ready to help us; as soon as we put away our weak **practices**, opportunities spring up on every hand to aid our strong resolve.

The world is our kaleidoscope, and the varying combinations of colors it presents to us at every succeeding moment are the exquisitely adjusted pictures of our ever-moving thoughts and **practices**.

AFTERWORD: AS YOU PRACTICE

The Effect of Thought and Practice on Health and the Body

The body is a delicate and plastic instrument, and responds readily to the thoughts by which it is impressed, and the **practices** it undertakes.

The body is the servant of the mind. It obeys the operations of the mind, whether they be deliberately chosen or automatically expressed.

At the bidding of unhealthy thoughts and **practices** the body sinks rapidly into disease and decay; at the command of glad and beautiful thoughts and the right **practices** it becomes clothed with youthfulness and beauty.

Disease and health, like circumstances, are rooted in our thoughts and everyday **practices**.

Out of a clean heart comes clean **practices**, comes a clean life and a clean body.

Thought and Purpose **(Destination)**

Thought allied with **practice** becomes a creative force...

Until conscious thought is linked with **practice** there is no intelligent accomplishment.

Aimlessness is a vice, and such drifting must not continue for those who would steer clear of catastrophe and destruction.

Those who have no central **destination** in their lives fall an easy prey to bad **practices**, fears, troubles, and weakness, all of which lead to failure, unhappiness, and loss, for weakness cannot persist in a power-evolving universe.

We need to conceive a great **destination** in our heart and mind, and set out to accomplish it.

We should make this purpose, this **destination,** the main focus in our lives.
When we devote ourselves to this attainment, not allowing ourselves to wander off the path, this is the royal road to self-control and true concentration of thought.

Even if we fail again and again to reach our **destination** – as we necessarily must until our weakness is overcome – the *strength of character* gained will be the measure of our *true* success, and this will form a new starting point for future power and triumph.

Strength can only be developed by effort and **practice,** and the soul believing this will at once begin to exert itself, adding effort to effort, patience to patience, strength to strength, will never cease to develop, and will at last grow divinely strong.

Having conceived of our **destination**, we should mentally mark out a straight pathway to its achievement, **a road map to follow**, looking neither to the right nor to the left.

Thoughts of doubt and fear never accomplished anything, and never can. They always lead to failure. Those who have conquered doubt and fear have conquered failure.

The will to do springs from the knowledge that we *can* do.

Thought and **practice** allied fearlessly to a **destination** becomes a creative force; those who *know* this are ready to become a master.

AFTERWORD: AS YOU PRACTICE

Thought and Practice as a Factor in Achievement

All that you achieve and all that you fail to achieve is direct result of your own thoughts and **practices**.

In a justly ordered universe, individual responsibility is absolute.

Your weakness and strength, your purity and impurity are your own, and not anyone else's; they are brought about by yourself and altered by yourself, never by anyone else. Your suffering and your happiness evolve from within.

As you think, and as you **practice**, so you are; as you continue to think and continue to **practice**, so you remain.

Stronger people cannot help the weaker unless the weaker are *willing* to be helped, and even the weaker must become strong of themselves; they must by their own efforts, develop the strength and **practices** that they admire in others. Only we can ourselves can alter our conditions.

We can only rise, conquer, and arrive at our **destination,** by lifting up our thoughts and getting to work. We can only remain weak and miserable by refusing to lift our thoughts and get to work.

Our worldly success will be directly proportional to the degree that we overcome selfish, indulgent **practices** and focus our minds on the development of our plans, and the strengthening of our resolution to **practice** and our self-reliance.

The universe does not favor the greedy, the dishonest, the vicious, even though for a while it may appear to do so; it helps the honest and the virtuous.

All the great teachers of the ages have declared this in varying forms.

Achievement, of whatever kind, is the crown of **practice** or effort. By the aid of well directed thought, resolution, and self-control we overcome laziness, lack of self control, and confusion of thought.

All achievement, whether in the business, spiritual, intellectual, or physical world, are the result of definitely directed thought, a defined **destination**, and everyday **practices**.

Those who would accomplish little must **practice** little; those who would achieve much must **practice** much; those who would attain highly must **practice** greatly.

Visions and Ideals

Those who cherish a beautiful vision, a lofty ideal in their hearts, will one day realize it … if only they **practice**.

The dreamers and the **doers** are the saviors of the world. The visible world is nourished and sustained by the beautiful visions and practices of its solitary creators.

Humanity needs to honor its dreamers and doers.

Composer, sculptor, painter, photographer, poet, prophet, sage, entrepreneurs, these are the makers of the world, the architects of heaven.

Those who cherish a beautiful vision, an ideal **destination**, with **practice**, will one day realize it. Columbus cherished a vision of another world, and he discovered it.

AFTERWORD: AS YOU PRACTICE

Cherish your visions; cherish your ideals; cherish the music that stirs in your heart, the beauty that forms in your mind, the loveliness that drapes your finest thoughts, for with the right **practices** they will grow into delightful conditions, and an amazing life; if you remain true to them, your world will at last be built.

The greatest achievement was at first and for a time a dream. The oak sleeps in the acorn; the bird waits in the egg; and in the highest vision of the soul a waking angel stirs. Dreams are the seedlings of realities, but everyday **practice** is how they become reality.

When you travel within, and do the inner work, you cannot stand without.

Whatever your present environment may be, you will fall, remain, or rise with your thoughts, vision, and **practices**. You will become as small as your controlling desire; you will become as great as your dominant aspiration.

The thoughtless, the ignorant, and the lazy, seeing only the apparent effects of things and not the **practice** behind the things themselves, talk of luck, of fortune, and chance.

Seeing someone grow rich, they say, "How lucky they are!"

Observing another become a renowned scholar, they exclaim, "How favored they are!"

They do not see the trials and failures and **practicing** that went on every day. They are not aware of the immense resistance that was overcome, the hours of undaunted efforts and sacrifices they put forth, the faith they exercised, that they might overcome the apparently insurmountable and realize the vision of their heart.

They do not know the long hours of **practice**, the darkness and the heartaches; they only see the light and joy, and call it "luck"; they do not see the long and arduous journey, they only see the end product and call it "good fortune"; they do not understand the process, but only perceive the result, and call it "chance".

In all human affairs there are **practices**, and there are *results*, and the strength of the **practice** is the measure of the result. It is not chance.

So called "gifts", powers, material, intellectual, and creative possessions are the fruits of **practice**; they are thoughts completed, objects accomplished, visions realized, **destinations** reached.

The vision that you glorify in your mind, the picture you sanctify of the **destination**, the ideal that you enthrone in your heart – this you will build your life by, and this you will become.

So, wherever you may be, under whatever conditions you may live, know this:

In the ocean of life the angels are smiling, and the sunny shore of your ideal **destination** awaits your coming. Keep your hand firmly upon the helm of thought and **practice**.

In the ship of your soul reclines the commanding Master – she does but sleep; wake her.

Self-control is strength; right thought is key; and right **practice** is mastery.

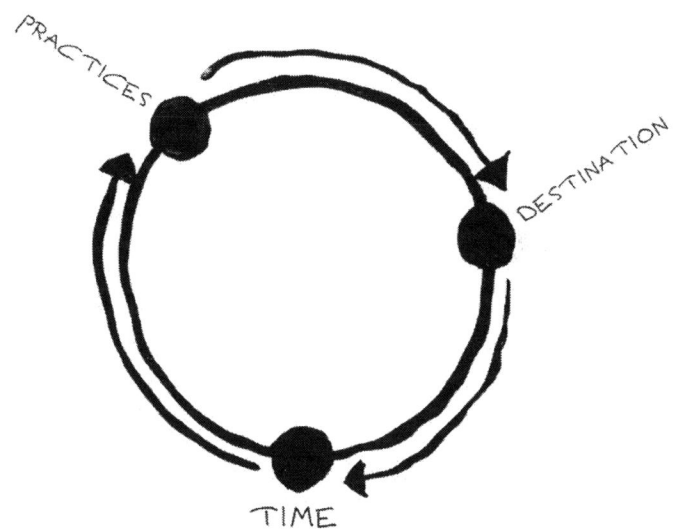

WORKBOOK

WEALTH PRACTICE

What is your ultimate destination? Where do you want to go? Where do you want to end up? Write it here or in your journal. Write it in as detailed a format as you can.

_____
_____
_____
_____
_____

What practices will get you there? If you don't know, study the paths of others and write them down here.

_____
_____
_____
_____
_____

What have you been practicing? How did you get here? List as many practices as you can. What did you practice today, this week, this month? Are these practices leading you to wealth or poverty?

_____
_____
_____
_____

VISION MAP

(draw a treasure map, writing out all your intended practices and steps to reach your destination. See example at the end of the book.)

I AM HERE

ULTIMATE DESTINATION

HEALTH PRACTICE

What is your ultimate destination? Where do you want to go? Where do you want to end up? Write it here or in your journal. Write it in as detailed a format as you can.

_____
_____
_____
_____
_____

What practices will get you there? If you don't know, study the paths of others and write them down here.

_____
_____
_____
_____
_____

What have you been practicing? How did you get here? List as many practices as you can. What did you practice today, this week, this month? Are these practices leading you to health or sickness?

_____
_____
_____
_____

VISION MAP

(draw a treasure map, writing out all your intended practices and steps to reach your destination. See example at the end of the book.)

I AM HERE

ULTIMATE DESTINATION

RELATIONSHIP PRACTICE

What is your ultimate destination? Where do you want to go? Where do you want to end up? Write it here or in your journal. Write it in as detailed a format as you can.

_____
_____
_____
_____
_____

What practices will get you there? If you don't know, study the paths of others and write them down here.

_____
_____
_____
_____
_____

What have you been practicing? How did you get here? List as many practices as you can. What did you practice today, this week, this month? Are these practices leading you to a great relationship or not?

_____
_____
_____
_____

WORKBOOK

VISION MAP

(draw a treasure map, writing out all your intended practices and steps to reach your destination. See example at the end of the book.)

I AM HERE

ULTIMATE DESTINATION

SKILL PRACTICE

What is your ultimate destination? Where do you want to go? Where do you want to end up? Write it here or in your journal. Write it in as detailed a format as you can.

_____
_____
_____
_____
_____

What practices will get you there? If you don't know, study the paths of others and write them down here.

_____
_____
_____
_____
_____

What have you been practicing? How did you get here? List as many practices as you can. What did you practice today, this week, this month? Are these practices leading you to mastery or mediocrity?

_____
_____
_____
_____

WORKBOOK

VISION MAP

(draw a treasure map, writing out all your intended practices and steps to reach your destination. See example at the end of the book.)

I AM HERE

ULTIMATE DESTINATION

DAILY PRACTICE
Let's look at your future. What did you do today?

Errors in judgment practiced every day lead to disaster/tragedy

A few disciplines practiced every day lead to greatness/mastery

EXAMPLE VISION MAP

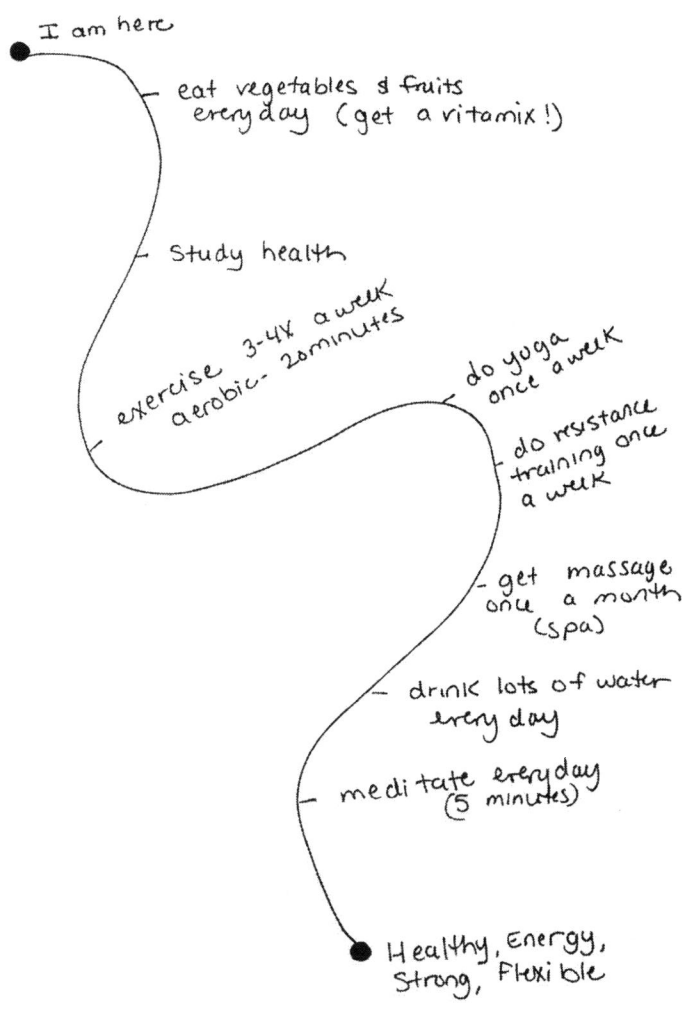

RESOURCES

FOR THE FULL WISDOM LIBRARY OF BOOKS AND RESOURCES THAT THE AUTHOR HAS STUDIED AND RECOMMENDS, VISIT:

www.10000hoursbook.com

ABOUT THE AUTHOR

GREW UP ON AN APPLE TREE FARM, RODE HORSES, PERFORMED MY FIRST BEETHOVEN SONATA BY AGE 12, DID A COVERGIRL AD AT AGE 15, MOVED TO NYC TO PURSUE MUSIC, GOT SIDETRACKED AND SIGNED WITH FORD MODELS, TRAVELED TO 25 COUNTRIES BY AGE 25, BOUGHT MY FIRST CAMERA AT AGE 17 IN TOKYO, LOVED, LOST, BECAME AN ARTIST, TRAVELED AUSTRALIA BY BUS FOR 3 MONTHS WITH CAMERA AND JOURNAL, BECAME A PAINTER AT 26, DIRECTED FIRST DOCUMENTARY ON CREATIVITY AT 33, FELL FOR A BRAZILIAN MAN, NEVER LEARNED TO COOK, INVENTED MY FIRST PRODUCT THAT ENDED UP ON OPRAH'S O LIST, LOVE READING BOOKS OF WISDOM, PASSIONATE ABOUT LEARNING, CREATED SECOND SUCCESSFUL COMPANY MAKING BOOKS FOR PHOTOGRAPHERS, LEARNED HIP HOP DANCING, GREEN TEA LOVER, LOVE TO WRITE IN JOURNALS, HIGHEST PURPOSE TO BE PRESENT, RIGHT NOW, EMPTY MIND, LIVE FROM SOUL, HERE TO DANCE EVERY DAY, PASSIONATE ABOUT LIVING LIVE FULLY, LOVE

www.phyllisophy.com

Made in the USA
Coppell, TX
16 February 2022